THE HEALTHY HOME

BEAUTIFUL INTERIORS THAT ENHANCE THE ENVIRONMENT AND YOUR WELL-BEING

JACKIE CRAVEN

First published in the United States of America by
Rockport Publishers, Inc.
33 Commercial Street
Gloucester, Massachusetts 01930-5089
Telephone: (978) 282-9590
Fax: (978) 283-2742
www.rockpub.com

Library of Congress Cataloging-in-Publication Data
Craven, Jackie
   Healthy home : beautiful interiors that enhance your environment / Jackie Craven.
      p. cm.
   ISBN 1-56496-939-8 (Hardcover)
   1. Interior decoration—Health aspects. I. Title.
   NK2113.C74 2003   2002007907
   613'.5—dc21

ISBN 1-56496-939-8

10 9 8 7 6 5 4 3 2 1

Design: Yee Design
Cover Image Courtesy of: R.O.O.M
Back Cover Images Courtesy of:
   Smith + Noble (top)
   Ikea (middle)
   Maine Cottage Furniture/Dennis Welch (bottom)

Printed in China

ACKNOWLEDGMENTS

As with any creative project, many people contributed to the making of this book. For reaching out to me and guiding me to this project, I am indebted to a most remarkable agent, Barbara Doyen. For their painstaking research assistance, I am grateful to Marjorie Corbett, Paula Kirman, and Laura K. Lawless. Most especially, I would like to extend my gratitude to the extraordinary team at Rockport Publishers, in particular to photo editor Betsy Gammons for her outstanding work in seeking out the images for these pages.

Finally, my awe and appreciation go to the many designers and thinkers whose work and ideas are reflected here. Their insight and creativity are the soul of this book. And, for their much-needed, ongoing encouragement and support, I offer a simple, heartfelt thanks to Susan Carroll Jewell and my special friends in the Arnold Madison Writers Group.

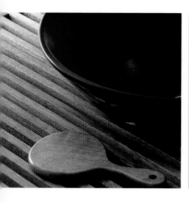

CONTENTS

DESIGNING FOR BODY AND SOUL

"Study nature, love nature, stay close to nature. It will never fail you."

Frank Lloyd Wright (1869–1959), U.S. architect

You know when you have entered a healthy home. Regardless of the period and style, there is a sense of harmony and purity that nourishes both body and soul. Over time, you may also notice that you breathe more easily, feel more content, and begin each day with heightened energy and enthusiasm.

One of the great ironies of our age is that the very technologies intended to enhance our well-being often undermine our health. Modern heating and cooling systems entice us with promises of temperature-perfect rooms, yet colds and allergies plague us. Chemical additives permit more durable paints, fabrics, wood, and construction materials, yet they fill the air with toxic fumes. Mass-produced synthetics and composite construction materials appear to save money, yet their ingredients trouble us with ailments ranging from mild headaches to severe depression. Ultimately, there is something unsatisfying about wrinkle-proof fabrics and laboratory-created walls and floors. Lacking the warmth and patina of materials drawn from nature, they sap our spirits in ways that are subtle yet profound.

The healthy home nurtures those who dwell inside and also protects the world beyond its walls. Designed with sensitivity for the environment, it is energy-efficient, economical, sustainable, and nonpolluting. Perhaps it resembles the eco-friendly houses that evolved as part of the popular "green architecture" movement of the 1980s and 1990s. Drawing from ancient building techniques, these homes are constructed of earth, clay, straw, or steel-reinforced concrete forms. Solar-powered and naturally cooled, they provide modern comforts without draining resources.

However, you need not set up housekeeping in a monolithic dome or an earth-sheltered dwelling to live in harmony with nature. Even the most traditional home, which may have been built long before the rise in environmental consciousness, can be adapted to incorporate the key principles of healthy design.

Hallmarks of a Healthy Home

PURITY

Nothing could be more essential to your health than the air you breathe, yet many of the most common household materials emit formaldehyde, benzene, trichloroethylene, and other hazardous chemicals. To some extent, installing a purifier with a HEPA (high-efficiency particle) air filter or ULPA (ultra-low penetration) air filter may control indoor air pollution. However, the best way to enhance air quality is to minimize the amount of toxins that are brought into the house.

In the healthy home, furnishings and finishes are drawn from nature. Organic cotton and linen are chosen above synthetic fabrics. Pure wood is preferred to furnishings made from pressed-wood products. Brick, stone, and tile are selected over vinyl. Biodegradable water-based paints, varnishes, and stains are used in place of oil-based products. Even the solutions used to clean the home are nontoxic and fume-free.

CONSERVATION

The healthy home is kind to the environment. For the most economical heating and cooling, rooms are arranged to capitalize on nature's rhythms. Appliances and lighting are selected for their energy efficiency. Plumbing fixtures are equipped with water-saving devices. Storage bins in the kitchen and utility rooms encourage users to recycle bottles, cans, and papers.

In living areas, environmental awareness brings an exhilarating freedom from excess and waste. Flexible floor plans permit rooms to take on multiple uses. Movable screens transform a spacious dining room into a private study. Many of the furnishings and decorative items are reclaimed from flea markets; others are constructed from salvaged timber. Even lampshades and wallpaper may be made from recycled paper. By conserving resources, occupants discover that their home and its contents take on special meaning. Reclaimed furnishings and handcrafted items are valued for their purity, simplicity, and artistry. Objects that were once disposable become treasures and heirlooms.

For Cleaner Air...

- Keep rooms well ventilated.

- Install exhaust fans in the kitchen and bathrooms.

- Change filters in heating and cooling equipment.

- Clear debris from stove and dryer vents.

- Use all-natural building materials and fabrics.

- Throw away plastic bags and bottles.

- Choose water-based paints and varnishes.

- Grow plants in water instead of soil.

- Clean frequently with natural solutions such as vinegar or lemon juice.

- Place printers and copy machines away from living areas.

- Eliminate tobacco smoke.

SIMPLICITY

The healthy home is easy to maintain. While rooms need not be spare, they are free of clutter, heavy fabrics, and bulky cushions and curtains. Collections are displayed with restraint. Woolen area rugs and rush mats take the place of wall-to-wall carpeting. Furnishings are often nonupholstered or covered with easy-to-wash cotton or linen slipcovers. The smooth, uncomplicated surfaces in these rooms make them inhospitable to dust, allergens, and microscopic dust mites and their droppings. In addition to preventing physical ailments, the simplicity in design yields deep psychological rewards: Living in clean, uncluttered spaces liberates the mind and lightens the spirit.

ERGONOMICS

"Ergonomics" is a term most often applied to offices, yet the furnishings and arrangements in every room should encourage patterns of posture and movement that promote musculoskeletal health. In the healthy home, kitchens are designed with accessible cabinets and efficient organization of workspaces. Bathrooms feature comfortably sized fixtures and easy-turn faucets. Bedrooms replace traditional pillows with cervical pillows and "bed wedges" to help prevent neck pain. Living areas are furnished with chairs that permit deep relaxation while providing proper support for the spine. Often overlooked details such as lever-handle door latches and touch-pad wall switches facilitate easy, stress-free movement through the house.

GREEN SPACES

Plants are not merely decorative. Growing abundantly throughout the home, they nourish the soul and reaffirm ties with nature. Some scientists believe that common houseplants even help purify the air. While the research is hotly debated, there is some evidence to suggest that certain species may actually absorb formaldehyde, benzene, carbon monoxide, and other harmful fumes. In the healthy home, at least two plants are placed per 100 feet of floor space. Rooms with unusually high ceilings receive additional greenery. To prevent mold spores (a common allergen), many of the plants are grown in water instead of soil. Window atriums and skylights contribute to interior green spaces and flood the home with nurturing sunlight.

Plants to Help You Breathe

- Bamboo palm
  (Chamaedorea seifritzii)

- Chinese evergreen
  (Aglaonema modestum)

- English ivy
  (Hedera helix)

- Gerbera daisy
  (Gerbera jamesonii)

- Janet Craig
  (Dracaena 'Janet Craig')

- Marginata
  (Dracaena marginata)

- Mass cane/Corn plant
  (Dracaena massangeana)

- Mother-in-law's tongue
  (Sansevieria laurentii)

- Pot mum
  (Chrysantheium morifolium)

- Peace lily
  (Spathiphyllum 'Mauna Loa')

- Warneckii
  (Dracaena 'Warneckii')

HEALING LIGHT

Bright, full-spectrum light manufactures vitamin D, regulates hormones, boosts the immune system, and wards off depression. The healthy home combines natural light with carefully chosen energy-efficient artificial illumination. To invite sunshine into the home, some windows may be free of curtains and shades. Others may rely on textured glass or bamboo screens to emit light while providing privacy. In some homes, innovative "smart windows" with electrically switchable glazings let homeowners adjust the opacity with a twist of a knob.

For artificial lighting, designers choose full-spectrum incandescent fixtures that imitate the sun's natural rays. Carefully placed mirrors help maximize the illumination; the subtle effects of color and shadow become a part of the overall design plan.

Richly colored, all-cotton bed linens combine with treasured artworks to transform a bedroom into a special place for relaxation and renewal.

OPPOSITE

*Tinted glass blocks and ceramic tile cast a
watery blue hue over a tub designed for luxurious soaking. Extra towels are stashed in a box
for easy storage in the linen closet, located
away from damp bathing areas.*

COLOR CONSCIOUSNESS

Nothing will affect the atmosphere of a room more than the color of its walls
and furnishings. Numerous studies have shown that specific colors will trigger a physiological and emotional response. Blue, for example, tends to lower
the blood pressure; red increases the heart rate. Some research suggests that
certain colored lights may aid in healing illnesses. However, every color has
subtle hues, and responses may be as individual as a fingerprint. Enlightened
designers select colors that best suit the purpose of the room and the personalities of its occupants. The flow of colors between rooms and the color
properties of artificial lights also come into play.

REFRESHING WATER

Five thousand years ago, healers used mineral water to treat disease. In the
fourth century B.C., the Greek physician Hippocrates prescribed therapeutic
baths. The ancient Romans transformed natural hot springs into elaborate
bath complexes to restore the body and the spirit. Today, doctors often
recommend hydrotherapy to ease the symptoms of arthritis, improve circulation, and relax sore muscles.

Drawing upon this wisdom, the healthy home makes room for luxurious
bathing areas with sensual tiled surfaces. Even a modest home may include
a chin-deep Japanese soaking tub in a separate area from the toilet and
bathing facilities. To assure water purity, a reverse osmosis water filtration
system works silently behind the scene. The filter's carbon block and ultraviolet light remove lead, bacteria, and other harmful substances commonly
found in municipal tap water.

SOOTHING SCENTS AND SOUNDS

Photographs cannot capture the complete experience of a healthy dwelling.
Upon entering these homes, you may be enveloped by sensations that stir a
deep sense of serenity. Wind chimes sing at an open window. Indoor fountains, often surrounded by fragrant flowering plants, echo the music of a
bubbling brook. Well-planned placement of furnishings and acoustical panels
orchestrates the flow of sound through the house. To add to the atmosphere
of calm, herbs and natural oils waft subtle aromas selected for their
medicinal powers.

SACRED SPACES

Decorated with love and sensitive to the environment, the healthy home is a temple for body and soul. More and more homeowners, regardless of their faith, are inspired to create private areas for reflection, meditation, and prayer. Highly personal artwork and icons give special meaning to home altars. Bedrooms and bathing areas also become sacred retreats designed for rest, restoration, and intimacy. Throughout the home, treasured collections thoughtfully displayed are both highly decorative and spiritually significant. Paintings and sculpture inspired by the traditions of many cultures are powerful reminders that we are all connected.

For the body...

- Free your home from toxins.
- Arrange furnishings and storage for comfort and ease.
- Remove bulky, dust-collecting cushions.
- Vent moisture from damp rooms.
- Create special places for exercise and relaxation.

For the psyche...

- Clear away clutter.
- Let in the sun.
- Choose mood-enhancing colors.
- Grow fragrant herbs.
- Fill rooms with soothing sounds.

For the soul...

- Provide quiet places for reflection.
- Replace throwaways with keepsakes.
- Strive for simplicity and moderation.
- Bring nature indoors.
- Honor the environment.

India

Vástu shástra, a part of *Sthapatya Veda,* seeks harmony through proper alignment of five life forces: space (ether), air, fire, water, and earth. To balance these energies, Vedic law prescribes the most beneficial placement and orientation for the home and its contents. The movement of the sun, stars, and planets helps determine design decisions.

 # China

Feng shui teaches that all things have a life force. This energy, called chi, must be balanced by harmonizing the elements of metal, fire, water, wood, and earth. Some *feng shui* practitioners follow ancient guidelines for the precise placement of furnishings in the home. Other practitioners use compasses and other instruments. Modern scientific ideas are often integrated with the old traditions.

 # Japan

Zen Buddhist ideals encourage the use of natural materials and simple forms. Stripped down to their bare essentials, rooms become serene spaces to escape trivial daily concerns and contemplate nature. Spacious and austere, Zen Buddhist design does not follow specific laws, but strives for a sense of spiritual openness.

HEALTHY ENERGY

The modern world swirls with hidden forces. Moving at 186,000 miles per second, high-energy electromagnetic waves bombard us from computer monitors, portable phones, microwave ovens, and hundreds of other gadgets we use every day. Some scientists suspect that chronic exposure to these electromagnetic frequencies (or EMFs) disrupts the functioning of calcium in the brain. Other researchers say EMFs interfere with the growth and reproduction of cells throughout the body. Regardless of the reasons, EMFs have been linked with health problems ranging from mental confusion to childhood leukemia, brain tumors, and other cancers. Although no research has conclusively proved these risks, enlightened designers are sensitive to ways electromagnetism may affect body and spirit.

Care is taken to place televisions at least five feet away from seating areas. Sleeping areas are located as far from electronic equipment as feasible. Metal bed frames and innerspring mattresses, which can attract magnetic forces, are avoided. The benefits of technological conveniences are weighed against their possible risks. In some cases, devices such as cell phones or microwave ovens may be removed from the home. In other cases, designers draw upon the wisdom of ancient Eastern philosophies to encourage a healthy flow of energy through the home.

EASTERN IDEALS

Vástu shástra, feng shui, and other Eastern philosophies are teaching designers how to create spaces that harmonize with nature and the forces of the universe. Rooted in Hinduism, *vástu shástra* is the inspiration for the elegant proportion and rhythm of India's magnificent palaces and temples. The ancient Chinese principles of *feng shui* draw upon Taoist philosophies to foster a harmonious flow of natural forces. Zen Buddhist philosophies originating in Japan combine with Chinese ideas to create a unique aesthetic based on balance, proportion, harmony and simplicity.

At the foundation of each of these philosophies is the understanding that all things in the universe are profoundly interconnected. A home decorated in accordance with ancient Eastern laws inspires a deep sense of inner peace because each detail is selected with loving concern for the whole.

THE WAY TO SERENITY

Within these guidelines, there are many paths to a healthy, harmonious home. For its clean open spaces and flexible floor plan, the Bauhaus penthouse may energize and nurture all who live there. Lovingly decorated with natural fabrics and furnishings, the suburban raised ranch may become a place of safety and restoration. The respectfully restored Queen Anne cottage may also represent enlightened design so long as it expresses loving care for the environment and provides for the physical, emotional, and spiritual health of its inhabitants.

Indeed, your first inkling that a home has been designed according to these ideals will not be its architectural style. Rather, you will know the health of the home by its refreshing beauty and the deep sense of serenity it inspires.

"Place is more important than strength."

Vedic proverb

ABOVE

Flickering candles and gleaming hardwood floors bring nature's glow to an urban space. Plant cuttings taking root in water help to freshen the air.

HEALTHY BEGINNINGS

Entrances are the first part of the home we see, and also the last. They are the sites of our comings and goings, greetings and farewells, beginnings and endings. With a door that offers protection and a foyer that comforts and shelters, this important space bridges the inner and outer worlds.

The state of the entryway will reflect the health of the home. If the entrance is orderly, serene, and aesthetically pleasing, then it soothes the spirit and allows the free flow of positive energy. However, if papers and handbags are piled in an untidy clutter and coats are crumpled on a chair and the space is poorly lit, then entering the home becomes a dispiriting act and a feeling of unease will work its way deeper into the home.

Houses often have more than one entrance. The front foyer, where guests are greeted, may be decorated to impress. However, family and close friends may routinely enter and leave the home through a dark, untidy garage or utility room where they are surrounded by garbage pails, garden tools, laundry hampers, or paint cans. The daily arrivals and departures through this dreary space convey the unspoken message that the people we most care about are unworthy.

Whether the door to the home opens into a formal entry foyer, a utility room, a kitchen, or a living room, the area at the threshold plays an important role in determining what goes into the house. Think of the entrance as a passageway for worldly possessions and also for ideas. Designing this space is a logical time to evaluate priorities and assess the importance of material objects. Step back and watch the daily patterns and preferences of your household from a detached distance. Take time to reflect on the overall aesthetics of the home and the beliefs and needs of your family.

There are no rigid rules for designing a healthy, eco-friendly home. Researchers offer suggestions and ancient Eastern philosophies provide guidelines, but no two people are affected to the same extent by allergens, synthetic chemicals, and electromagnetic energies. Moreover, each of us will respond differently to sensory details such as color, light, temperature, and aroma. In the end, you may need to rely on your instincts and a keen sense of observation. As you create your design plan, listen closely to your inner voice.

"Into the house where joy lives, happiness will gladly come."

Japanese proverb

Passageways
to Health

- Clear the entryway of clutter.

- Create ample storage.

- Keep the area well lit.

- Provide a chair or bench and a place to set shoes.

- Choose colors that harmonize with the exterior and the interior of the home.

- Use living plants to soften sharp corners.

- Change water in fountains and aquariums often.

- Use mirrors to draw in restful scenes and to redirect negative energy.

- Select artworks or collections that affirm family values.

- Add fresh, natural fragrances.

- Hold a formal house blessing ceremony.

- Place a symbol of peace and protection at the door.

Clear the Space...

In the healthy home, both the formal and the functional entrances are given equal importance. Begin by emptying the space completely. Clean out storage areas, sweep away dust, and wash floors and shelves with lemon-scented water. Decide what items are necessary and what needs to go. Pack up the nonessentials and give them to friends or charities. With clutter removed, the entryway will feel larger and more inviting.

To keep passageways clear, you will need to be something of an anthropologist. Watch the routine activities of your family and observe where the debris of daily living tends to accumulate. Notice the tables that collect unruly piles of mail; look for chairs that are turned into hat racks and coat trees. Design the entryway not merely to impress visitors but to accommodate the way your family actually lives. By providing appropriate storage, you will not only free the space of blockages but also help keep clutter from making its way further into the home.

If the entryway has a closet, optimize that storage space by adding easy-to-reach hooks and a lower pole for children's coats. Use sturdy wooden hangers for heavy garments and put a jute mat or a cotton throw rug on the floor for boots. Consider storing out-of-season items elsewhere in the house.

For entryways that do not have closets, you may want to add an armoire, a chest of drawers, or cabinets to stow belongings out of sight. To give utility rooms a fresh, uncluttered appearance, install doors on open shelves. Provide decorative canisters for umbrellas, wooden trunks for sports equipment, and fabric-lined baskets to catch gloves, scarves, and sunglasses.

Creative strategies for storage will be especially important if the home does not have a clearly defined entryway. When the doorway opens directly into a living area, there is the risk that sweaters will end up on sofas, keys on the kitchen counter, and mail-order catalogs on the dining table. To help maintain order, place beside the door a small table with drawers, bowls, or baskets to catch keys, mail, and school supplies. Use coat trees and wall hooks for coats, sweaters, and scarves. Children will be encouraged to put their belongings away if they have their own special hooks and baskets labeled with their names or an identifying color.

"Have nothing in your houses that you do not know to be useful or believe to be beautiful."

William Morris (1834–1896), English craftsman and designer

In a simple home without an entry foyer or hall closet, a small table and wicker baskets help catch clutter at the door.

ABOVE

Bright colors invite visitors to sit and slip off their shoes in this uncomplicated entryway. The enamel pot catches keys and other knickknacks.

Create Harmony...

So much of what goes into the making of a healthy home is not seen but sensed. The quality of the light, the freshness of the air, and the invisible energies profoundly influence our physical, emotional, and spiritual well-being. Ideally, the entryway will establish a warm, welcoming atmosphere and provide a smooth, peaceful transition into the home.

DEFINE THE SPACE

An entryway that opens abruptly into the living area may be unsettling for persons in the room and also for new arrivals. Try setting up a translucent screen to mark the boundaries of the entrance area. If space is limited, use area carpets, lighting, and a subtle shift of colors to ease the transition.

SOFTEN THE EDGES

In keeping with the principles of *feng shui,* strive to create a space that feels expansive. Sharp corners or a series of open doorways can create discord at least on a subconscious level. Similarly, a blank wall facing the door will seem cold and forbidding. Without adding clutter, you will want to incorporate details that soften the space. Consider placing a fish tank or a small fountain near the threshold. A miniature garden of raked sand, a potted Warneckii plant, or a Chinese evergreen will evoke nature and help establish a sense of calm. A well-placed mirror will pull restful views into the room.

THINK ABOUT COLOR AND LIGHT

As with every part of the home, color and lighting are crucial to setting the tone. To ensure harmony, seek colors that coordinate with the exterior of the house and reflect the aesthetics of interior rooms. Make sure that the entry is well illuminated with nonglaring ambient lighting. Fanlights or transoms over the door will add cheerful natural sunlight. So that no one has to fumble in the dark, place a lamp or switch directly by the door, or use a motion sensor or automatic timer.

> "Before you prepare to improve the world, look around your own house three times."
>
> **Chinese proverb**

DISPLAY COLLECTIONS

The entryway sets the stage, and also seals the memories. This is an ideal place to display artwork, photographs, or collections that reflect the personalities and values of the family. Beware, however, of over-exuberance. One or two items prominently displayed will have more significance than an extensive collection. For the most meaningful displays, be sure to select like objects: Instead of assorted figurines, choose several blue porcelain birds.

FURNISH SPARELY

The fewer furnishings placed in the entryway, the better. Provide a chair or bench so that visitors can easily sit and remove their shoes, and, if needed, a small table or chest to catch keys and other small objects. Any element that might inhibit the flow of energy should be softened or, if possible, removed.

RIGHT

Soothing green hues and artwork that evokes nature help to soften the angular corners of a stairway. Muddy footsteps can't harm the ceramic tile flooring.

Clear the Air

Aromas are subtle. Even without our awareness they will trigger memories and evoke strong emotions. An entryway that passes through a utility room is likely to contain paints and other products that emit toxic vapors. A garage is certain to contain a high level of combustion byproducts. Any entrance can assault the senses if the home includes synthetic wall-to-wall carpeting, composition wood furnishings, and other products with chemical additives.

The heavy fragrances of commercial air fresheners only compound the problem because they are made with chemicals that can cause fatigue, depression, and other ailments. Use furnishings and finishings made of all-natural materials instead. An air purification system will help remove toxins, and some scientists believe that common houseplants such as bamboo palm or chrysanthemum also cleanse impurities from the air.

To freshen a room naturally, bring in vases of flowering lavender or small sachets of cedar chips. Or, fill small bowls with an essential (pure) oil from aromatic plants such as sandalwood or sage.

"The wise traveler leaves his heart at home."

African proverb

For Air Purity

Installed on your furnace, in your ductwork, or freestanding, an air filter will help cleanse pollutants from your home. Some filters remove particles; others help remove gasses. For the greatest degree of air purity, you will need to install both types of filters, or use a filter that incorporates more than one system.

Particulate Filter
Your furnace probably already has a fiberglass or polyester filter that removes larger particles from the air. It is inexpensive and easy to maintain, but it does not remove smaller particles or gasses.

Medium Efficiency Extended Air Filter
A pleated filter with a larger surface area catches more particles than a standard furnace filter. Medium efficiency filters trap nearly half of all particle matter but cannot filter out gasses.

High Efficiency Particle Air Filter
Known as HEPA filters, these powerful air purifiers are often used in hospitals. Cigarette smoke and nearly all particles are removed from the air. Because a large motor is required, a full-scale HEPA filtration system is seldom used in private homes.

Electrostatic Particulate Filter
The friction of air moving through the filter creates static electricity, and larger particles are trapped. Although it will not trap smaller particles, an electrostatic filter is very helpful for removing pollen and mold spores.

Electrostatic Precipitator (Ionizer)

Mounted into your ductwork, an ionizer turns dust into magnets and then draws it to metal collector plates. Large proportions of particles are trapped, but the filter needs frequent cleaning.

Turbulent Flow Precipitator

Particles are caught in a whirlwind of moving air and then dropped into a containment space. TFP filters are efficient for removing particles; they do not filter gasses.

Activated Carbon Filter

Carbon granules absorb heavier gasses. Lighter gasses such as formaldehyde are not affected. The filter must be changed often, or pollutants will be released back into the air.

Activated Alumina Filter

Even lighter gasses like formaldehyde are absorbed and destroyed by the activated alumina material. Many manufacturers offer combined alumina and carbon filters.

Room Filters

Small, freestanding filters let you cleanse the air without installing a major air filtration system. These portable devices operate a variety of ways, including activated carbon, activated alumina, and HEPA filtration. The larger the air filter, the more effective it will be.

ABOVE

A polished branch directs the flow of energy in a narrow hall. The runner is earth-friendly woven sisal.

Talismans and Charms

Beautiful objects invested with mystical powers become the focal point for doorways and entrances into a comforting home.

Mojo Bag
Many African cultures believed that bags filled with spices, teeth, feathers, and other objects from nature embodied special powers. The Mojo (luck) bag became charged with magic by blessing it according to traditions of the tribe.

Sand
In some cultures, a jar of sand on the windowsill or doorstep was thought to trap harmful spirits. The spirits become so absorbed in counting the grains, they never enter the house.

Glass Globes
This tradition uses enchantment to ward off evil. Globes of spun glass hanging in the windows dazzle the wandering spirits, thus preventing them from coming inside.

Dzi Beads
More than a thousand years ago, peoples in Tibet etched intricate designs onto polished agates. These lovely beads became known for their mystical powers.

Buddhist Talismans

Small pieces of yellow cloth are painted with a picture of Buddha and inscribed with sacred writings from Buddhist scriptures.

Taoist Talismans

Also made of yellow cloth, these symbolic emblems contain mantras from the I-Ching and are traditionally written with blood from a chicken, dog, or human.

Pentagram Patterns

From ancient Egyptian icons to modern-day police badges, the five-pointed star is one of the most common symbols for bravery and protection. Interwoven with intricate designs, the pentagram becomes a talisman that is both beautiful and potent.

Jewish *Mezuzah*

A tiny scroll is inscribed with sacred text affirming devotion to God and describing the divine duties of the family. This is placed inside a *mezuzah,* or small case, and hung on the doorframe. Many people of the Jewish faith practice the custom of kissing the *mezuzah* when they enter and leave the home.

Invoke Safety and Protection...

Through the ages, the peoples of many cultures have used talismans and charms to ward off evil and invoke special powers. The earliest talismans were crafted from plants and animals that suggested qualities of strength or courage. For example, ancient tribes from many parts of the world believed that the antlers from a deer or the foot of a swift animal would help tribe members escape danger. Over the centuries, mankind adopted increasingly complex symbols to represent power and protection.

Placing a talisman or lucky charm on the door or near the threshold is not mere superstition. In addition to their appeal for divine assistance, these symbols inspire feelings of safety and reflect the values of the family. Because they reach deep into our minds and touch archetypal memories, talismans can be powerful sources of psychic and spiritual energies. Choose traditional symbols drawn from your own religion, or create images that speak to your deeply felt beliefs. Hang a wreath of healing herbs or stencil comforting words and patterns on the door. Any object can become an emblem of security if it resonates for you and your family.

OPPOSITE

Golden hues and gentle curves create a smooth, peaceful passageway into the home. The cheerful illumination comes from flickering sunshine mingled with ambient lighting along the ceiling. Hanging ornaments and a woodcarving serve as talismans, inviting good fortune.

"We should learn from the snail: It has devised a home that is both exquisite and functional."

Frank Lloyd Wright (1869–1959), U.S. architect

HEALTHY LIVING AREAS

"The wise man and the tortoise travel but never leave their home."

Chinese proverb

There is a loose, organic feel to living areas that are healthy. An open, uncluttered floor plan encourages free movement and frees the spirit as well. This is a fluid, flexible space where family and friends gather, play games, and watch television or listen to music. The space may flow without boundaries into the dining room and kitchen, forming a single large "great room" which is the social center of the home.

While bedrooms and special purpose rooms may be custom-tailored to the particular needs of one or two persons, the living area must foster the well-being of an entire family, adapting to differing personalities and interests as well as varied requirements for physical comfort. In addition, the living area must accommodate a multitude of visitors, from drop-in neighbors to business associates to intimate friends. More than in any other room in the house, it is important to avoid introducing elements that might cause unrest for some users. Ideally, the colors, lighting, fabrics, and floor plan will welcome and comfort all who enter and will also inspire sociability and a sense of cooperation.

Flexibility is the key. For an airy atmosphere, choose lightweight furnishings that can be easily rearranged to meet the needs of the moment. Bring rattan chairs and a folding chaise in from the patio. Add sectional couches that may be separated and regrouped. Instead of a single large table, choose small modular tables that can be placed together or used individually. Free up additional floor space by stowing frequently used items in racks or shelves along the walls. Adjacent to the dining area, hang ceramic mugs and copper soup ladles from decorative hooks and set serving platters on the top of low bookcases.

Because so many people use this space, ergonomic design becomes especially important. A healthy living area will provide for visitors whether they are short or tall, slight or husky, young or old. Include a few chairs that can be adjusted for height and for angle. A reclining chair and a footstool will prove more comfortable than a traditional sofa. Plump cushions may appear inviting, but overstuffed furnishings seldom offer enough lumbar support to be comfortable for extended sitting or reclining. Moreover, a bulky, immobile sofa will appear ponderous and oppressive in this relaxed, free-flowing space.

A Japanese tatimi *mat, a low wooden table, and a touch of nature are all that's needed to create a soothing space for quiet entertaining. Limiting the palette to green and white enhances the serenity.*

Ancient Wisdom

For the emotional well-being and physical comfort of all who enter the living room, consider principles set down in ancient Eastern philosophies.

Feng Shui

- Provide plentiful sunlight.

- Avoid clutter.

- Display pictures and artwork that are meaningful to the family.

- Choose round, wooden tables.

- Arrange seating in a circle or octagon.

- Leave enough space around tables and chairs for easy movement.

- Enclose the television inside a cabinet. Do not make it the focal point of the room.

- Be wary of dead space in empty corners. Use color, up-lighting, and plants to move the flow of chi.

Vástu Shástra

- Fill the space with bright, nonglaring illumination.

- Use white and pastel colors on most walls.

- To encourage positive energy, consider painting the southern wall a deep maroon.

- Choose artwork that evokes pleasing thoughts.

- Avoid large obstructions in the center of the room.

- Avoid placing chairs beneath heavy beams.

- Place the heaviest furnishings in the southwest portion of the room.

- Place televisions and other electronic equipment in the southeast corner of the room.

Light, Airy, and Clutter-free...

For a light, airy atmosphere, choose pale colors in neutral tones. Barbara Richardson, director of color marketing at the Glidden paint company, suggests warm beiges and soothing grays for living areas that will be used by many people for many different purposes. Off-whites are relaxing and also adaptable. To add a splash of excitement, toss brightly colored pillows on the floor and focus accent lighting on a carefully chosen artifact.

Books, paintings, and decorative items bring warmth and personality into communal spaces. They express the interests and values of the family, evoke pleasant thoughts and memories, and stimulate conversation with visitors. However, as ancient Eastern philosophies suggest, these items should be displayed with restraint. Rather than crowd shelves with an entire collection, choose a few favorite items and change the exhibit every few weeks. To minimize dust and mold, enclose books in cases with glass doors.

For many families, the living area has become a home theater with television and stereo equipment dominating the room. The presence of so many electronic devices can have a draining effect on all who enter. Even when the machinery is turned off, it will emit electromagnetic waves, which have been associated with a variety of health problems. Moreover, the silent presence of a large, gray glass screen creates an air of desolation and draws attention away from human-centered activities.

To minimize the effects of electromagnetic waves, choose equipment that is classified as *low emission* and make sure that the wiring is properly connected. Store the television inside a cabinet and place seating at least five feet away. Be sure to close the cabinet doors when the TV is not in use.

> "Pictures deface walls more often than they decorate them."
>
> **Frank Lloyd Wright (1869–1959),**
> **U.S. architect, writer**

ABOVE

Pie sections of a modular table shape themselves for many uses. Water-grown plants and natural stone flooring add to the uncomplicated beauty.

Brimming with Life Energy...

If a family member or frequent visitor suffers severe allergies, there may be a temptation to design sterile spaces that are spotlessly clean but devoid of life. However, the healthiest living areas are not hospital rooms. With cascading ivy on the windowsills and a dog or cat snoozing in the sunlight, these rooms brim with life energy. Growing the plants in jugs of fresh water instead of soil helps minimize the growth of mold spores that could trouble allergy sufferers. Keeping animals well groomed and avoiding heavy carpeting help keep the air free of fur and dander.

In most cases, inviting life into the living room brings more health benefits than risks. Flourishing plants enliven the dead space in corners, circulate oxygen, and help freshen the air. The presence of a beloved dog or cat eases stress and, according to numerous research studies, increases longevity and enhances the physical and psychological well-being of the keeper.

While avoiding clutter, you may want to pull serene natural scenes into the living area by creating an indoor landscape with a peace lily and palms, polished stones and shells, and time-gnarled scraps of driftwood. Symbolizing prosperity and good fortune, a miniature fountain will add the soothing sounds of trickling water.

OPPOSITE

A soaring palm and a loving pet bring healing life energy into the home. Easy-wash cotton chair cushions and area rugs make sharing your home with a cat easier for allergy sufferers.

Living with Pets

Even if you suffer allergies, you can invite a dog or cat into your home. If possible, spend time with the animal before adopting it; you may be able to find a breed that does not cause you trouble. Then, to assure the comfort of allergy-sufferers, follow these guidelines:

- Keep fresh air circulating in the room.

- Use an air purifier with a HEPA filter.

- Change filters in purifiers, furnaces, and air conditioners often.

- Avoid wall-to-wall carpeting.

- Drape a towel or cotton throw over the pet's favorite nap spots.

- Vacuum area rugs, upholstery, and curtains frequently.

- Use slipcovers that can be quickly removed and laundered.

- Avoid using cat litter that is dusty or scented.

- Make bedrooms off-limits for pets.

- Bathe the cat or dog weekly in distilled water.

- Feed the pet a high-quality diet; healthy animals produce less dander.

Earth-friendly…

By blurring the boundaries between indoors and out, the healthy living area provides a life-affirming and welcoming space where family members and visitors of all ages can gather in love and community. In keeping with this spirit, health-conscious designers choose earth-friendly furnishings and fabrics that do not drain natural resources or add harmful pollutants to the environment.

As much as possible, choose flooring made of all-natural materials such as hardwood, slate, or ceramic tile. Area carpets may be woven from pure wool, organic cotton, or untreated hemp. For slip covers and window shades, use 100 percent cotton or linen. For furnishings, choose hardwoods that have been finished with water-based urethane or paint.

Many homeowners are tempted to buy "wrinkle-proof" textiles and "scratch-proof" manufactured flooring because these materials are perceived to be economical and trouble-free. Unfortunately, all synthetics emit fumes that can cause symptoms ranging from mild fatigue to severe depression.

The worst offender is wall-to-wall carpeting made of synthetic fibers. Because the carpeting is attached to the floor, allergy-aggravating dust and dust mites become trapped underneath and cannot be removed. Moreover, the synthetic fibers, padding, and adhesive all contain toxins that will take weeks to dissipate. Lingering fumes can trouble persons with serious chemical sensitivities for years.

Synthetic materials and chemical additives are so prevalent in the products we buy, it would be impossible to remove them entirely from a typical home. However, we need only touch the raised grain of solid oak or smell the fresh scent of sun-dried cotton to know that seeking out earth-friendly materials is an act of love, and well worth the effort.

"Simplicity of life, even the barest, is not a misery, but the very foundation of refinement: A sanded floor and whitewashed walls and the green trees, and flowery meads, and living waters outside."

William Morris (1834–1896), English designer, writer, painter, and craftsman

OPPOSITE

Subtle cove lighting supplements natural illumination in a scenic dining area. Chairs with graceful, swooping lines encourage the smooth flow of energy between the inner and outer worlds.

Earth-Friendly Fibers

The most beautiful and most durable fabrics are created without synthetic compounds. Choose plant fibers that have been responsibly harvested with a minimum of synthetic pesticides. Animal fibers should be gathered humanely, without slaughter.

Cotton

Soft and airy, cotton is harvested from the seedpod of the cotton plant. Because the fiber is hollow inside, cotton stays cool in hot weather and also dries quickly. Many manufacturers blend synthetics with cotton to make it more wrinkle-resistant. However, the softly crumbled appearance of natural cotton has its own rustic beauty. For the most eco-friendly fabric, look for all-natural organic cotton that has been grown without chemical fertilizers or pesticides.

Linen

Durable and refined, linen is made from flax, the same type of fiber used for clothing and shrouds in ancient Egypt. Linen fabrics are at least twice as strong as cotton, and they actually grow softer and lovelier after repeated washings. The natural wax content in flax gives linen a natural luster that is beautiful in its natural cream tones or richly dyed. Although linen wrinkles easily, it also irons easily and will long outlast synthetic imitations. Linen is also an earth-friendly fiber: Every part of the flax plant is used, leaving no waste.

Hemp

Grown in most of the temperate and tropic regions of the world, hemp is a shimmering, beautifully textured fiber made from stems of hemp plants. It wrinkles easily, but is highly water-resistant. Grown in Central America, sisal is an attractive kind of hemp frequently used for woven floor coverings. Mountain grass is a rich brown kind of hemp grown in China. Fabrics made from hemp may be as rugged as burlap and denim, as soft as cotton, or as delicate as silk and lace.

Ramie

Spun from an East Asian plant, ramie is a lustrous, white fiber that may be mistaken for linen. Ramie is twice as strong as flax and up to five times stronger than cotton. This wondrous fiber is also very resistant to bacteria and molds.

Jute

Strong and heat resistant, jute is made from the woody bark of the jute plant. Because it is inexpensive, it is often used as backing on carpet and linoleum.

Coir

These coarse, strong fibers are harvested from coconut husks, softened in seawater, and then pounded and combed. Hand woven in rustic weaves, coir is an economical and earthy floor covering.

Sea Grass

Grown in China, sea grass is a durable, stain-resistant fiber made from reed-like plants. Woven sea grass is a hard, durable floor covering.

Silk

These steel-strong, sensuously smooth fibers are woven from the cocoon of the silkworm. The silkworm secretes sericin, a glue-like substance which acts like a natural sizing. Lustrous and elegant, silk holds its shape and forms shimmering cascades when draped from windows. Because it is highly absorbent, silk can be dyed to intense, vibrant colors.

Wool

The same plush fibers that bring warmth to sheep, goats, camels, llamas, rabbits, and other animals are woven into long-wearing, dirt-resistant fabrics for upholstery and carpeting. Wool fibers are slightly kinked, and fabrics made of wool will spring back into shape after being creased. Although some wool feels scratchy, many are extremely soft. For sensual smoothness, choose downy camel hair, cashmere from the Kashmir goat, or mohair from the Angora goat. As you shop for specialty wools, be mindful of conservation efforts. Avoid the very rare variety made from vicuñas, because these beautiful members of the Llama family are killed to obtain their fleece.

Simplicity is key in a dining area designed for flexibility and functionality. The lightweight Shaker chairs have seats woven from twine-like twisted sea grass. The long pine table accommodates relaxed dinner parties or eat-and-run family buffets.

Light Your Home without Draining Natural Resources

Make the most of natural daylight:

- Keep windows clean.

- Avoid heavy curtains and shades.

- Trim trees or bushes away from windows.

- Choose white, cream, and pastel colors for walls and furnishings.

- Hang mirrors.

Supplement the sun with energy-efficient lighting:

- Focus brighter lights on high-activity areas.

- Use lower wattage bulbs for soft, indirect illumination.

- Use lamps with 3-way switches; adjust light levels as needed.

- Install dimmer switches. Incandescent lights are less efficient when dimmed, but they last longer and use less wattage.

- Avoid chandeliers with many small bulbs. A single large bulb will provide more illumination for the same wattage.

- Use light colored, translucent lamp shades.

- Place some lamps in corners; the light will reflect off the walls.

- Wipe dust from light bulbs.

- Turn off lights when not in use.

Bathed in Sunlight...

Flickering over linen cushions, casting rippling shadows over polished oak floors, sunlight brings richness and depth to earth-inspired rooms. Natural light from the sun is also essential for our health and emotional well-being. When sunlight enters the eyes, it reaches the pineal gland and activates the endocrine system, which is connected to our immune and nervous systems. Without sufficient sunlight, we could not survive.

Sunshine is not only healthy; it is free. When the sun is used for most daytime lighting needs, electricity is spared and our natural resources are conserved. This does not mean, however, that we should strip away all curtains, cut skylights into our ceilings, and fill our rooms with nonstop illumination. Unfiltered sun is likely to produce uncomfortable glare and may also overheat the home. At night, blank black windows will chill the room and the spirits of all who come there. In most homes, some type of window treatment is necessary.

> "The sun at home warms better than the sun away."
>
> **Albanian proverb**

Energy-Efficient...

Begin by observing the path of the sun. Spend a full day in the room and make note of the movement of the light with the passing of the hours. Move catlike through the space to locate the warm, comforting spots. Arrange seating to capitalize on bright, energy-free illumination for reading. Avoid arrangements that would force seated persons to squint directly into the glare. Also be sure to move the television out of direct sunlight.

As needed, soften the sun with light-filtering bamboo blinds or sheer curtains made of cotton gauze. Venetian blinds with wooden slats will let in direct beams of light with a single pull of a string. Keep in mind that any window treatment with multiple slats will tend to collect dust and will require extra maintenance. To minimize the need for cleaning, the Pella Corporation has developed retractable shades sandwiched between double windowpanes. Several other manufacturers offer a variety of "smart windows" that have special glazing or film to control heat and light. New advancements in "switchable glazings" have created glass that operates electrically, letting you change the illumination, heat, and level of privacy with the turn of a knob. Of course, installing windows with this type of technology does mean introducing more electrical activity into a room that may already be overwhelmed by a television, a stereo, and other equipment.

OPPOSITE

Bamboo blinds provide natural, light-filtering privacy in this sunny living area. The recessed ceiling lamps may be brightened or dimmed as needed. The unobtrusive table lamp is equipped with a three-way switch for soft background illumination or brighter task lighting.

Smart Windows

Photochromic
Like sunglasses that darken when you move into bright light, photochromic windows respond to changes in light. As the windows darken, glare is reduced. Although they block light, photochromic windows do not reduce heat.

Thermochromic
In the sun's natural heat, thermochromic glass turns white and reflective. Solar heat is also reduced, saving air-conditioning costs. When thermochromic glass is reflective, vision is completely obscured, making this technology impractical for standard windows.

Liquid Crystal
Two layers of film enclose a layer of tiny liquid crystals. Turn the electric current on, and the window becomes slightly hazy but transparent. Liquid crystal windows provide privacy, but do not save energy: The glass admits the same amount of light and solar heat whether it's on or off.

Electrochromic
Flip a switch and an electric field signal alters the window's optical and thermal properties, changing the glass from clear to fully darkened or any level of tint in between.

The Many Shades of Light

Standard Incandescent

A small coil of tungsten wire produces a warm, golden glow. Incandescent bulbs are the most common form of lighting for private homes and also the least efficient. Long-life incandescent bulbs last longer but use more energy.

Neodymium Incandescent

Made with glass that contains the rare element neodymium, these incandescent bulbs imitate the soft, natural color tones of sunlight. However, neodymium incandescents do not produce the true ultraviolet light needed for optimum health.

Tungsten Halogen

These incandescent bulbs have tungsten wires heated by halogen gas. They produce brighter, whiter light than standard incandescent bulbs.

Reflector Lamps

Ideal for spotlighting and down-lighting, reflector lamps are incandescent fixtures that disperse the light over specific areas. Mirrors inside the fixture focus the illumination.

Low-Voltage

These lamps use less current than standard lamps. A transformer in the fixture reduces the voltage to the required level. Low-voltage halogen lamps are extremely hot and can be hazardous if not handled correctly.

Fluorescent

An electric current courses through mercury and inert gas in a tube or a compact bulb. Fluorescent bulbs last at least ten times longer than incandescents, and they are much more energy-efficient. However, some researchers are concerned that low frequency radiation generated by the bulb and the transformer may be detrimental to one's health.

Full-Spectrum Fluorescent

Typically, fluorescent lighting casts an unnatural yellow-green glow. Bulbs with a higher Color Rendering Index (CRI) show colors more accurately. Full-spectrum fluorescent lamps simulate the full range of colors, including ultraviolet. The result mimics that of natural sunlight.

> "All architecture is shelter, all great architecture is the design of space that contains, cuddles, exalts, or stimulates the persons in that space."

Philip Johnson, U.S. architect

Full-spectrum Lighting…

As daylight wanes, the most uplifting and eye-soothing effect is achieved by combining natural illumination with soft background lighting and brighter task and accent lights. For energy efficiency, plan a flexible lighting scheme that can be easily adjusted when activity in the room changes. Lamps with three-way switches will let the user choose the amount of illumination needed. Dimmer switches alter the atmosphere instantly and extend the life of incandescent bulbs.

Many energy-conscious designers are choosing highly efficient fluorescent lighting. The older fluorescents so often used in offices and schools produced a glaring yellow-green hue and emitted a steady low hum. Newer fixtures are quieter and register colors more accurately. Full-spectrum fluorescent lighting actually simulates the complete range of natural sunlight, including the ultra-violet light our bodies need to manufacture vitamin D. The crisp white glow of full-spectrum lighting resembles outdoor lighting at noon. Persons who suffer from Seasonal Affective Disorder (SAD), which is triggered by a lack of sunlight, find speedy relief when they spend time in rooms illuminated by full-spectrum fluorescents.

Unfortunately, all fluorescent lighting, including full-spectrum lamps and compact fluorescent bulbs, emit low levels of electromagnetic radiation. Before replacing existing fixtures with full-spectrum fluorescent lighting, you may want to seek more natural ways to bring lighting into the home.

Some incandescent bulbs also claim to simulate sunlight. Made with neodymium glass, they produce a pleasing white illumination that is soothing and appears quite natural. However, these bulbs cannot capture the full spectrum of colors rendered by sunlight, and they do not provide any of the health benefits found in full-spectrum fluorescent lamps.

One of the most pleasing forms of energy-efficient artificial lighting may be found in low-voltage halogen lamps. Used in track lighting and wall sconces, they cast soothing pools of white light, making them ideal to accent an artwork, illuminate dark corners, or provide nonglaring light over the dining area.

For soft, natural atmospheric lighting, flick off the electricity altogether: Let large candles made of naturally scented wax fill the living and dining areas with a golden, gently flickering glow.

HEALTHY KITCHENS

"Food is our
common ground,
a universal
experience."

James Beard (1903–1985),
U.S. chef, author

In the not-so-distant past, many cultures placed the messy, smoky cooking areas away from the main living quarters. The kitchen was located in an outbuilding, a basement, or a separate wing cordoned off by a heavy door. In this way, family members were protected from fumes, greasy vapors, and fire hazards.

Yet, rooms where food is prepared speak to fundamental human needs for warmth and nurture. Who among us has not been lured by the scent of baking bread, drawn by the happy chatter of the cooks, and enticed to linger near the warmth of the stove? Designed for the emotions and the spirit as well as the body, the healthy home integrates the kitchen with the primary living space, creating a free-flowing floor plan that accommodates work, play, and socializing. At the hub of family life, the kitchen is the soul of the home.

The kitchen is also the control center, buzzing with the energy of mechanical equipment, electrical devices, and technological wonders. The very machinery that brings comfort and convenience may also sap environmental resources, create health hazards, and evoke a sterile, industrial atmosphere. Designing the healthy kitchen begins with introducing soulful, earth-loving elements. Modern machinery need not be hidden behind cabinets, but it should be softened with details drawn from nature. Baskets of fresh fruit or ruby-bright jars of preserves are an appealing complement to glimmering white or shimmering black. Fruit-inspired colors, selected for their power to stimulate the appetite, also bring vitality to rooms where streamlined metallic appliances dominate. Splashes of deep red stimulate brain activity and increase respiration and pulse. Orange brings energy and aids digestion, lemon-fresh yellows suggest the sun, and blues and greens evoke calming thoughts of sky, trees, and fields.

Even the simplest details speak to the subconscious and transform a cold space into a room that is warm and nurturing. To soften electromagnetic energies and freshen the air, place potted herbs on the windowsill and rooting hyacinth beside the sink. Fill the room with the mood-enhancing scents of grapefruit and lavender. Let the babble of an indoor fountain muffle the mechanical hum of the refrigerator.

Designed for Comfort and Ease

Introducing warmth to the kitchen areas does not mean adding bric-a-brac, fussy curtains, or other heavy-handed details. The healthy kitchen finds its beauty in unpretentious functionality. Each item has a purpose and a place, and each design decision is made with careful attention to comfort and ease of use.

Many homeowners enjoy the efficiency of a U-shaped floor plan. A center island provides plentiful workspace and creates extra storage space below. Counters at varying heights allow users to stand or sit. However, you do not need to undertake a major remodeling project to create an ergonomic work area. Improving the comfort of your kitchen may be as easy as placing a sturdy table in the center of the room.

Whether the kitchen is equipped with state-of-the-art cabinetry or homey wicker bins, the storage must be logical and intuitive. Organize your equipment according to task and store each item close to where it will be used: mixers and bowls near the refrigerator, pots and spatulas near the stove, cleaning supplies and coffeemaker near the sink. Hang everyday pots and utensils in a glittering array from easy-to-reach hooks. Install rotating carousels and swivel racks in corner cabinets. To minimize bending and back strain, stow heavy items in pullout compartments and deep drawers with full-extension slides. To save steps, place the refrigerator and food cupboards adjacent to the door where groceries are brought in. An entry porch or vestibule may do double duty as a traditional "cold room," providing energy-free storage for perishables.

Some tasks normally associated with the kitchen may take residence in an entirely different part of the home. A beverage pot or a juicer and a small refrigerator will enhance the comfort of a bedroom, office, or spa. The patio or garden can become an outdoor cook center with a gas-fired wok, a wood-fired stove, and a soapstone sink. In turn, activities not related to food preparation may come to roost in a kitchen that is lovingly designed. Creative planning can transform an empty corner or a recess under the counter into a child's play nook, a family computer center, or a laundry area.

"A crust eaten in peace is better than a banquet partaken in anxiety."

Aesop, Fables

OPPOSITE

A rolling cart makes an instant island in a relaxed, flexible kitchen. The wrought iron candelabra doubles as a pot rack, keeping cooking essentials in easy reach.

Vástu Shástra

Because the family caregiver spends so much time in the kitchen, it must be lovingly planned. *Vástu shástra* wisdom tells us to pay close attention to safety, comfort, convenience, ventilation, lighting, temperature, and pest control.

- Health is enhanced when the cook faces east; place the stove in a southeast corner.

- Open windows on opposing walls for cross-ventilation.

- Do not place shelves directly over the stove.

- Choose woods, metals, and fabrics for their ability to soothe energies in the room.

 ## *Feng Shui*

For the health of the entire family, it is essential that the cook feel calm and centered. *Feng shui* wisdom tells us to carefully consider the placement of each appliance. The stove is especially important because it symbolizes health and wealth.

- Keep the stove clean, and make sure all the burners receive equal use.

- Provide uncluttered workspace around the stove.

- Place a mirror over the stove so that you can see who is entering the room.

- Place the stove so that it does not face the main door, the bathroom, the bedroom, a staircase, or a corner.

- Water puts out fire; do not place the sink near the stove. Place green, leafy plants between the stove and the sink.

OPPOSITE

At the heart of this relaxed kitchen is a solid spruce table with uncluttered space for dining or hobbies. A low-voltage pendulum lamp provides energy-efficient task lighting.

"Where love sets the table food tastes its best."

French proverb

LEFT

An efficiently planned kitchen becomes the center of household care. The compact, energy-saving laundry machines leave space for an uncluttered sewing counter and ample storage.

Conservation in the Kitchen

- Use rags and cloth towels instead of paper.

- Use cloth napkins and place mats.

- Use covered dishes instead of plastic wrap or aluminum foil.

- Replace paper with reusable mesh coffee filters.

- Keep recycling bins near where cans and bottles are used.

- Put lids on pots; they'll heat more efficiently.

- Put smaller pots on smaller burners.

- Avoid aerosols; the cans cannot be reused or recycled.

- Buy products packaged in recycled containers.

- Buy in bulk; larger items use less packaging.

- Avoid Styrofoam; it cannot decompose.

- Use a chalkboard to post family messages.

- Buy concentrated juices; they use less packaging.

- Compost vegetable scraps.

- Fix drippy faucets.

Designing for Safety

Creating a room where so much activity will occur is fraught with risks. The caring designer becomes something of a psychic, anticipating the many possibilities for accidents and incorporating ways to prevent them. Counters and cabinet corners are rounded to prevent bruises. Drawers are equipped with stops to prevent contents from spilling onto the floor. Safety latches keep knives and electrical appliances from children's reach.

The cooking equipment essential to a kitchen means that electrical shocks and burns are always a concern. Each large appliance should have a separate circuit wired directly into the main electric panel. To prevent shocks, outlets near sinks and dishwashers must be equipped with ground fault interrupter (GFI) circuits. Stoves and ovens are ideally located away from doorways. The thoughtful placement of wall ovens assures that users will never have to bend or reach to remove a heavy roasting pan. A burn-proof surface next to the stove provides a safe place to place hot pots.

The electrical gadgetry found in most modern kitchens poses another risk that may be subtle, but which some researchers say can be profound. The microwave, toaster, food processor, blender, garbage disposal, radio, clocks, and countless other small appliances all emit electromagnetic radiation. By clearing clutter from your countertop, you may help eliminate potential hazards and will, at the very least, minimize the psychological static caused by unnecessary electrical devices. Switch to a nonelectric can opener, use a hand whisk to whip cream, and throw away the electric carving knife. Simple tasks that don't require labor-saving devices are calming and more satisfying when done manually.

As an added precaution, use the microwave oven sparingly and stand away from it when it is in use. Refrain from standing by the stove for long periods. Set coffee pots and other appliances along walls which do not abut living areas. Unplug small appliances when they are not being used.

Air Purity

Researchers estimate that in a single year of normal kitchen use, about 200
pounds of greasy vapor, smoke, and moisture are spewed into the air. The
most common mistake in kitchen design is to neglect the venting and air filtration systems. A ducted hood with a charcoal filter can reduce grease and
odors, but it will not remove heat or moisture. Fungus and bacteria in the
ductwork reduce the efficiency of the fan and cause additional health hazards. Exhaust fans are more effective when they vent to the exterior of the
house. Better yet, windows and skylights provide energy-free ventilation and
plentiful natural illumination.

Another important step in improving air quality is to eliminate commercial
cleaning products. Detergents, ammonia, glass cleaners, bleach, cleansers,
and dish soap create potent fumes that linger on floors, work surfaces,
and dishes for weeks and months. Natural ingredients such as baking
soda, vinegar, and lemon juice will keep the kitchen squeaky clean without
polluting the environment.

Ideally, the place where we prepare food will be in harmony with nature
and all surfaces will be free from artificial compounds that outgas toxic
chemicals. Many kitchen cabinets manufactured today are constructed of
fiberboard, plywood, particleboard, and other compositions with formaldehyde-emitting glues. Frequently these materials are coated with a finish also
containing formaldehyde. To avoid toxins, install cabinets made of solid wood
and finished with a water-based coating. For a streamlined, high-tech kitchen,
consider steel with a brightly colored baked enamel finish. If new cabinets are
not an option, a coat of an alcohol-based primer/sealer will lessen the fumes.
The unhealthy fumes from manufactured woods dissipate after about ten
years, so older cabinets should not pose a problem.

Vinyl and the materials used to install it may also undermine air quality.
The healthiest floors evoke earth and water. Wood, stone, and clay-based
materials are comforting underfoot and do not pollute the air. Make sure that
any mortars or adhesives used in the installation are water-based and nontoxic.
Sealants and finishes should also be fume-free.

Orange and yellow are energizing and also help to stimulate the appetite. Brightly colored cotton table linens bring cheer and also help preserve natural resources.

> "Better than a banquet some- where else is a good cup of tea and a bowl of rice at home."

Japanese proverb

Earth-friendly Floors

Linoleum
Made from clay, cork, wood flour, linseed oil, resins, and pigments, linoleum is biodegradable, making it a more earth-friendly choice than vinyl. However, the linseed oil does emit an odor, especially when the linoleum is new.

Cork
Harvesting cork does not harm the tree; only the bark is used. When composed into floor tiles, cork takes on a variety of patterns in rich, earthen tones. The surface absorbs sound, insulates, and is resilient underfoot. A coat of wax or polyurethane may be needed to retain the sheen. The floor will dent under appliances and furniture.

Tile
Ceramic and porcelain tile that has been glazed during firing is almost impervious to stains and marks. Unglazed tile will show scuffs and must be sealed at least once a year. Tile made from recycled auto glass is strong and comes in a bright rainbow of colors.

Natural Stone
Limestone, slate, terra-cotta, sandstone, travertine, marble, and granite each has its own special appeal. Some stones evoke rugged mountainsides; others suggest grand palaces. All are hard, strong, and durable. Non-glossy, slip-resistant surfaces are best.

Hardwood
Oak, cherry, pine, and maple bring warm, lustrous beauty to any room. For rich colors and beautiful marble textures, also consider teak, kempas, and other responsibly harvested tropical woods. With several coats of a strong, nontoxic finish, wood will hold up well under moderate traffic and occasional spills. However, it may warp or buckle under dishwashers and other areas where there are frequent water overflows.

Bamboo
This steel-strong grass is more durable than many hardwoods, and finishes to lush golden or brown hues. Bamboo plants mature in three to five years, making them a quickly renewable resource.

Antique & Reclaimed Wood
Antique plank flooring and salvaged lumber conserves natural resources and enriches the kitchen with Old World charm. Since the wood is already trafficked and aged, it may prove forgiving of heavy wear.

Recipes for Healthy Cleaning

All-purpose Cleaner
Mix salt and vinegar in a spray bottle. Or dissolve 4 tablespoons baking soda in 1 quart water.

Coffee Pots and Tea Kettles
To remove mineral deposits, fill with white vinegar and let set overnight.

Disinfectant
Use two spray bottles. Spritz the area with white or apple cider vinegar. Also mist the area with 3 percent hydrogen peroxide. Rinse with water.

Garbage Disposal
To deodorize, grind chunks of orange, lemon, lime, or grapefruit.

Drains
To clear clogs, first use a plunger. Then pour in 1 or 2 cups baking soda followed by 1/2 cup white vinegar. Cover tightly for 1 minute. Rinse with hot water. Repeat in 30 minutes if needed.

Floors
For brick or stone, mix 1 cup white vinegar and 1 gallon water. For vinyl or linoleum, add a capful of baby oil. For wood, polish with a mixture of equal parts baby oil and vinegar.

Garbage Pails
To inhibit bacteria, sprinkle in 1/2 cup borax.

Laundry
Use borax in place of detergent.

Metals
- Aluminum: Polish with cream of tartar mixed with water.

- Brass: Mix lemon juice with baking soda or vinegar with salt. Polish using a soft cloth.

- Chrome and Tin: Polish with a paste of baking soda and water.

- Copper: Boil tarnished items in water with 1 tablespoon salt and 1 cup vinegar. Or try solutions using baking soda, cream of tartar, or lemon juice.

- Pewter: Mix a paste of salt, vinegar, and flour. Polish with a soft cloth.

- Silver: Line a pan with aluminum foil. Fill with water and add 1 teaspoon baking soda and 1 teaspoon salt. Submerge the tarnished silver item and bring to a boil.

- Stainless Steel: Wipe with undiluted white vinegar.

Odors
Place small dishes of vinegar around the room. Or add cinnamon, cloves, nutmeg, or vanilla to a pot of simmering water.

Ovens
Mix 1 part vinegar with 4 parts water. Spray onto cool oven and wipe with scrubber pad. Use baking soda on stubborn spots.

Pots and Pans
Scrub with salt and warm water.

Sinks
Scour with 2 tablespoons baking soda mixed with 1 pint warm water. As needed, add lemon juice or vinegar to cut grease.

Windows and Glass
Mix 2 or more tablespoons of vinegar with 1 quart of water. To reduce streaking, add cornstarch to the mixture.

Wood Cabinets and Furniture
Mix vinegar with olive oil or baby oil.

There's no need to hide the garbage pail: For color and style, use a sturdy steel container with a self-closing lid. A removable steel liner makes cleanups easy.

Lever-handled faucets are easier to operate for children and persons with disabilities. A tall gooseneck spout provides extra sink room.

Control Pests Without Poisons

First, seal any cracks where pests may enter. Then, try these home remedies:

- Cockroaches: Sprinkle borax mixed with sugar near openings.

- Ants: Sprinkle talcum powder, cayenne pepper, paprika, damp coffee grounds, bone meal, charcoal, chalk, or lemon juice with bits of the rind.

- Flies: To trap flies, coat strips of construction paper with honey. To repel flies, plant pots of mint or basil.

- Fruit Flies: Set out small dishes of vinegar to attract and drown the tiny fruit flies.

- Mice: Block holes with steel wool. To discourage mice from entering, soak cotton balls with pure peppermint extract and place around the house.

Clean, Natural Work Surfaces

Environmental tests show that kitchen sinks, countertops, and cutting boards are breeding grounds for bacteria such as E-coli and salmonella. Essential to the healthy kitchen is an area dedicated to hand washing, with a ready supply of fresh, easy-to-reach towels. Take special care to select a smooth work surface that will not absorb food spills and germs. Avoid plastic laminates and acrylic or polyester "solid surface" materials; they contain toxic substances. Wood brings natural warmth, but butcher-block counters may be prone to bacterial growth, especially if not regularly washed and sealed. Ceramic or porcelain tiles with a high gloss glaze are strong, scratch-proof, and scrubbable, but joints and grout lines may trap food spills if not carefully sealed.

For maximum cleanliness, many health-conscious homeowners are turning to high-tech metals and innovative new materials. With its bright silvery sheen, stainless steel is easy to wash, rinse, and sanitize. Copper, zinc, and brushed nickel offer the benefits of steel with a softer patina. Crafting surfaces from frosted or tinted tempered glass evokes an aura of spaciousness. The glass may show sticky fingerprints, but is quickly polished to a squeaky-clean sheen. Recent developments in fabricated concrete are creating rock-hard work surfaces with heatproof finishes. The illusion of a pebble-strewn beach may be evoked by polished bits of glass and stones imbedded in the concrete.

However, for its power to evoke nature, no material can equal earth-born granite, slate, marble, and other stones. Spewed from volcanoes, formed in riverbeds, and quarried from mountains around the world, stone suggests timelessness and solidity. With colors ranging from creamy flesh tones to mossy greens to ebony, these are sensual surfaces that partner perfectly with wood, ceramic, glass, or metal.

OPPOSITE

Electric gadgetry is not necessary for simple tasks like squeezing juice. Hand-powered tools are both beautiful and functional.

Earth-Quarried Countertops

Granite

Impervious to water and difficult to scratch, granite will hold its richly hued sheen for many years. Acidic spills, like lemon juice, vinegar, red wine, or cola, should be wiped up immediately to avoid surface dulling.

Kirkstone

Quarried in the hills of the Lake District in England, this sea-green rock is formed from volcanic ash and is almost as hard as granite.

Lavastone

Born in the volcanic flows of Volvic, France, and enameled with a jewel-bright, diamond-hard finish, lavastone is impervious to heat and impermeable to water, grease, and acids. It is commonly known by the brand name Pyrolave.

Marble

With creamy swirls of color, marble evokes the aura of an Old World palace. Its smooth cool surface is ideal for rolling baking dough. However, marble is softer than granite, and easily scratches, chips, and stains. The pink or yellow lime-stone, called travertine, resembles marble and also needs some special care.

Slate

Deep-hued and shimmering, slate resists acid stains and will hold up under hot pots. Use steel wool to buff out scratches.

Soapstone

Although soft, soapstone is easy to maintain because scratches can be quickly buffed out with light grit sandpaper. As it ages, the grayish blue patina will darken to a rich charcoal shade.

Creamy whites and subtle splashes of color enhance the beauty of charcoal granite.

According to feng shui *wisdom, the potted sunflowers stabilize energies in the room.*

Energy Efficiency

REFRIGERATORS

The greediest consumer of home energy is the refrigerator. It should never be enclosed inside unvented cabinets or placed beside the stove or other hot appliances. The heat will make the compressor work harder, draining power. An empty freezer also has difficulty maintaining cold temperatures; keep it at least two-thirds filled. For optimum efficiency, keep refrigerator coils clean, turn off the "exterior moisture" switch, and choose a moderate temperature setting.

When purchasing a new refrigerator, select a model that has the freezer compartment on the bottom. It will use less energy than a side-by-side model, and food used most frequently will be in easy reach. Some high-efficiency refrigerators and freezers are divided into compartments that can be opened separately, conserving cold air in unopened compartments. Also, watch for new developments in electronic refrigerator and freezer control systems. The eco-friendly kitchen of tomorrow may include refrigerators and freezers made with electrochromic glass so that users can see inside without opening the doors. Several European manufacturers are creating models that recycle their own waste heat and combine refrigeration, freezing, and household warming in a single function.

OVENS

In most cases, gas uses less energy than electric. Newer stoves with pilotless ignitions are highly efficient because the thermal igniter does not operate continuously while the oven is on. However, the energy savings of cooking with gas may not be worth the health risks. Gas can emit high levels of nitrogen dioxide, which may cause respiratory problems for some users. In terms of air purity, electric is a better option.

For energy-efficient electric cooking, consider installing a convection oven. A fan circulates air inside the oven for more even distribution and reduced cooking time.

ABOVE

A compact "clothes processor" washes and dries in the same drum, saving both space and energy.

COOKTOPS

Electric ceramic cooktops are easy to clean, and also economical. Many come with dual circuit elements. To conserve energy, heat smaller pots using only the smaller inner circle. Induction cooktops are faster and more efficient than gas. Because they use electromagnetic energy to heat magnetic material in the cookware, the cooking surface magically stays cool. There is no heat loss, and less chance of accidental burns.

DISHWASHERS

Dishwashers are not mere self-indulgences; the high heat kills germs. For maximum efficiency, look for a model with a built-in booster heater for sanitation during the rinse cycle. Also make sure the dishwasher has variable wash cycles and an air-dry option. To save both energy and water, the New Zealand-based company Fisher & Paykel has developed a convenient "DishDrawer" dishwasher with two separate drawers for smaller loads.

LAUNDRY

To conserve water, choose an "H-axis" washing machine that uses tumbling instead of agitation to clean clothes. Make sure your model offers cold water and small load settings. Look for washers with two water in-flows, one for hot water and one for cold, allowing the use of water heated externally to the machine through non-electric means. The German manufacturer Foron makes machines that actually recycle water from the last rinse.

For clothes drying, select a model with a moisture sensor; the dryer will shut off automatically when the laundry is done. Better yet, consider a super-efficient European-style "clothes processor" that washes and dries inside a single drum. When weather permits, treat your linens to sun-kissed warmth: Hang them outside to dry.

> "Sharing food with another human being is an intimate act that should not be indulged in lightly."
>
> M. F. K. Fisher (1908–1992),
> U.S. culinary expert, author

HEALTHY BEDROOMS

Even in the largest homes, most of us spend a third of our lives in a single room. Sleeping and dreaming, we restore our bodies and our psyches. Engaging in quiet conversation and making love, we touch both our spiritual and our primal selves. Our physical and psychological health hinges on what happens here.

Recognizing the importance of the bedroom, many designers are creating large, elaborate spaces that indulge the senses and satisfy every whim. The master bedroom may become a self-contained oasis with a kitchenette, a sophisticated entertainment center, and a whirlpool tub. However, your sleeping area need not be palatial in order to be healing. In fact, over-exuberant decorating intended to inspire fantasy and romance often runs counter to the principles of healthy design.

Ideally, our places of restoration and intimacy should be secluded from the noise and commotion of family life. In homes with open floor plans, such as a studio apartment, loft, or *tatami* room with no dedicated space for sleeping, use sliding screens, tall Ficus plants, or other visual cues to ease the transition between day and night activities. If the bedroom contains a home office or a television, these distractions should be obscured as much as possible. In many cases, a judicious use of light, color, mirrors, and decorative details will help draw the boundaries between the waking and the sleeping worlds.

Deep relaxation requires a release from inhibitions. Many of the principles of ancient Eastern philosophies address the importance of safety and a sense of protection in the bedroom. *Vástu shástra,* for example, warns against placing a bed beneath a beam. *Feng shui* suggests locating the master bedroom as far from the front door as possible. To enhance feelings of security, *feng shui* wisdom also advises that we place furnishings in an octagonal arrangement, with the bed at one corner. According to the traditions of many cultures, placing a talisman such as a Native American dream catcher at the bedside encourages restful sleep. Symbols that speak to the psyche help release anxieties.

"The beginning of health is sleep."

Irish proverb

Simple Comforts...

Beds can be deceptive. A cloud-soft mattress piled with pillows and festooned with velvet or tapestry suggests luxury and romance. Yet this type of fairy tale bed is more likely to stir nightmares than inspire pleasant dreams.

The healthiest bed is an uncomplicated affair. With a firm mattress, it supports the spine without creating uncomfortable pressure points. With a flat or cervical pillow, it follows the natural curve of the neck. An adjustable back or wedge-shaped cushion allows a comfortable posture for nighttime reading. Bulky covers and curtains, more for show than functionality, are avoided because they tend to trap dust and harbor the microscopic dust mites that thrive there. For a truly restful sleep, you may need nothing more than a well-chosen futon or an adjustable chaise placed in a serene and private part of the home.

The pineal gland requires a period of pitch darkness to promote sleep-inducing melatonin. If street lamps tend to shine into the room at night, be sure to provide light-blocking window shades. Also, pay special attention to the types of illumination used in the bedroom. Harsh overhead lights are not conducive to sleep or romance. Consider adding dimmer switches to existing fixtures, table lamps for indirect illumination, and small book lights for reading in bed. Lamps with colored shades will cast a therapeutic glow: To ease insomnia, bask in blue-tinged light.

Although we cannot see them or hear them, the currents emitted by electrical devices may be as disruptive as light or noise. Designing sleeping areas that are genuinely restful may mean removing some of the conveniences we take for granted. Choose a separate area for watching television and keep electrical clocks and radios away from the head. If electromagnetic waves are a concern, be wary of beds that have metal springs; over time, they will acquire a slight electrical charge. Use beds with wooden slats or woven jute supports, and place them as distant as possible from electrical equipment. If appliances are located in an adjacent room, avoid placing the bed against the opposite wall.

Where to Put the Bed?

For the most restful sleep, be sure to place the bed in a location where you feel completely secure. The ancient traditions of *feng shui* offer these guidelines:

- Keep sleeping areas distant from the main entrance to the house.

- Arrange the bed so that the foot does not directly face the door or a mirror.

- Make sure that you can easily see the door when seated in bed.

- Allow one side of the bed to touch a wall.

- Place the headboard slightly away from the wall.

- Know your health and longevity directions; use them to guide placement of the bed.

"The way you prepare the bed, so shall you sleep."

Yiddish proverb

ABOVE

A wooden chaise with an adjustable back
adapts for sitting or sleeping. Choose synthetic-
free cotton canvas for cushions and carpeting.

Healthy sleeping areas begin with natural fabrics and chemical-free cleaning. To prevent dust and allergy-aggravating dust mites, give bed linens plenty of fresh air and bright sunlight.

"Every man is a prince in his own bed."

Malawian proverb

Naturally Soft...

The bed is the most intimate of furnishings. Its covers touch every part of our bodies, embracing us in sensuality and in sleep. While we want to avoid plush mattresses and pillows that do not support the spine and neck, we need warmth and tenderness.

Unfortunately, most of the bedding sold today is not healthy. Permanent press sheets are treated with formaldehyde and other toxic chemicals. Covers made of inorganic polyester blends release fumes that may interfere with breathing, disrupt sleep, and lower resistance to disease. Even cotton bedding is not safe if the fibers were grown with pesticides.

Instead of synthetics, choose organically grown 100 percent cotton or cotton kapoke, a resilient, lightweight fiber harvested from the silk cotton tree. The term "organic" means that the fiber was produced without pesticides or chemical fertilizers and was not treated with chemical bleaches, dyes, or surface finishes. The strongest, softest, and most luxurious cottons are Egyptian, grown in the Nile River basin, and Pima, grown in the southwestern part of the United States. Regardless of the cotton you choose, look for the highest possible thread count. A higher thread count creates a tighter weave and a softer, more durable fabric.

Other natural choices for healthy, luxurious bedding include pure silk and, for blankets, some varieties of pure wool. Feathers and down make plush, chemical-free stuffing for pillows and quilts, but they may cause problems for allergy sufferers.

Even if you cannot replace all your linens with 100 percent pure, organically grown fibers, you can create a healthier, more restful sleeping area simply by choosing a detergent that does not contain perfumes, phosphates, or other factory-made chemicals. Most commercial detergents are not biodegradable. They pollute the environment, irritate the skin, and interfere with breathing. Simple baking soda or untreated soap is safer for our rivers and streams, and also gentler on our bodies.

Laundry Tips

- Use 1 cup borax, plain baking soda, or flakes from pure bar soap to clean a load of clothes.

- To prevent colors from fading, add a few drops of vinegar to the laundry water.

- To brighten whites, pour in an extra cup of borax, or a cup of food-grade hydrogen peroxide.

- Treat stained linens with salt and vinegar; hang them in the sun to bleach.

- To minimize wrinkles, make sure fitted sheets cover the bed snugly.

- Iron pillowcases with water that has been naturally scented with lavender.

Coping With Dust Mites

- Keep clutter and knickknacks out of the bedroom.

- Keep surfaces dust-free.

- Avoid upholstered furniture; use wooden chairs.

- Choose simple, easy-to-clean window treatments.

- Avoid wall-to-wall carpeting.

- Damp-mop floors frequently.

- Use a vacuum cleaner with a HEPA filter.

- Wash bedding often in hot water.

- Place mattress on a slatted wood base, or use a futon.

- Expose mattress to fresh air; roll, fold, or turn it frequently.

- Keep humidity low: Remove sources of moisture and use a dehumidifier.

- Change filters in heating, cooling, and air purifiers.

Dust-free...

Frequent cleaning is important in sleeping areas because bedding is especially prone to dust mite infestations. Feeding off the dead skin that sloughs naturally from our bodies, these microscopic organisms breed in sheets, blankets, pillows, and carpeting. Their droppings are responsible for much of the respiratory discomfort associated with dust.

It would be impossible to remove dust mites completely from the home, but preventative measures will help reduce their populations. Because it cannot be pulled up and laundered, wall-to-wall carpeting is best avoided. If you feel you must have carpeting to insulate a cold floor or to muffle noise, make sure the room is vacuumed often using a cleaner with a HEPA filter.

Allergen-impermeable covers will help thwart mite infestations in pillows and mattresses. However, these covers generally contain polyester and other synthetic products that can cause skin irritations and other problems. A healthier solution is to simply wash linens often in hot water and expose bedding to fresh air as much as possible. As a final line of defense, be sure to clear the bedroom of dust-collecting clutter; stow personal items in closets, cabinets, and drawers.

"No sleep, no dream."

Korean proverb

ABOVE

A strategically placed mirror pulls pleasant views into the room. Simple lines and muted colors evoke a sense of order and calm.

Clutter-free...

For many families, the bedroom is also the dressing room and the grooming room. It can quickly collect tangles of belts and shoes, odd bits of pocket change, and assorted clutter that catches dust and disrupts relaxation and romance. Providing ample storage is an important step in reducing anxiety and fostering a sense of calm.

A popular solution is to stow belongings in bins under the bed or beneath skirted tables. Although these solutions do move clutter out of sight, the items may continue to prey on the consciousness, and will certainly make it difficult to vacuum and dust under furniture. A better resolution is to eliminate all but the most essential possessions and to store necessities in closets, armoires, bureaus, and cabinets with closing doors. A trunk at the foot of the bed, a storage bench beneath the window, and a table with drawers will help prevent the unwanted display of distractions. A commercial closet organizer can be enormously helpful; however, do make sure that the shelves are not made of plastic, pressboard, or other toxin-emitting synthetic materials.

Closet Cleanup

- Empty the closet completely.

- Wash the floors, walls, and shelves. For a fresh scent, add lemon juice to your wash water.

- Discard misshapen and broken clothes hangers.

- Try on all clothing. Discard any item that does not fit.

- Reflect on the importance of each belonging. Discard any item that you are not likely to use.

- Divide clothing according to season: Summer, Winter, and Spring/Autumn.

- Set aside accessories and miscellaneous items that do not fit in any one category.

- Fit closet with shelves and storage bins. Pest-proof cedar will help keep clothing fresh.

- Install double-decker poles for shirts, jackets, and other short items.

- Hang a shoe rack on the back of the closet door.

- Provide drawers or bins for belts and scarves.

- Select an appropriate hanger for each item.

- Store out-of-season clothing in an out-of-the-way location.

- Group clothing according to purpose; hang work clothing together for easy access.

- Fold bulky sweaters and store on shelves.

- Place formal clothing inside zippered bags.

- Give discarded clothing to charities.

ABOVE

Organizing the closet helps free the mind and opens life for new possibilities. Well-planned shelves, drawers, and clothes racks can transform a single wall into an orderly storage area.

> "It's better to sleep on the floor in an incense shop than in a bed in a fish market."

Vietnamese proverb

Sensual...

Freed from the absent-minded accumulation of knick-knacks and clutter, the healthy bedroom makes way for true love and uninterrupted dreams. It speaks to the senses through color and candlelight, fresh flowers, healing fragrances, and soothing silence.

Choose colors for their softness and their restful properties. Pale green relieves anxiety, stimulates the immune system, and promotes harmony, hope, and serenity. Powder blue lowers the blood pressure, decreases the heart rate, and encourages sleep. Violet is calming and spiritual, while mauve and pink suggest love and romance.

Aromas trigger long-lost memories, touch the emotions, and inspire dreams. To fill the room with healing life energy and fresh natural fragrances, set small pots of flowering bulbs on the windowsill. If allergies prevent bringing plants into the sleeping area, use dried herbs, naturally scented candles, or massage oils and lotions. Experiment and observe closely the ways aromas affect your body and mood. By selecting sensual details that resonate for you, you tap into the subconscious—where all healing begins.

OPPOSITE

A healing light flows through a room draped with sheer white cotton.

If You *Must* Have Carpeting...

Health-conscious designers avoid wall-to-wall carpeting because the thick fibers trap dust, dust mites, and pollutants. Also, synthetic carpeting, carpet padding, and carpet adhesives emit chemical fumes that can cause a variety of health problems. However, the warmth and softness of a plush rug under the bed may be difficult to resist. For healthy carpeting, follow these guidelines:

- Choose carpeting made of pure wool or other all-natural materials.

- Ask your dealer for carpeting that is certified to have low-VOC (volatile organic compound) emissions.

- Make sure that the carpet padding is also certified low-VOC emissions.

- Install the carpeting without adhesives.

- Ask the dealer to roll out the carpet and pad in a ventilated area for a day or two before installation.

- Purchase the carpeting in mild weather. Keep windows open during the installation and leave them open for several days.

- If you are highly sensitive to fumes, plan to stay away from home for several days after the carpet is installed.

- Vacuum the carpets at least once a week; use a cleaner that is equipped with a HEPA filter.

- Avoid rug shampoos that contain synthetic chemicals.

- Treat carpeting once a year with a carpet sealant solution designed to reduce VOC emissions.

Healing Fragrances

Beyond the pleasing effects of their aroma, the oils from flowers, fruits, grasses, leaves, roots, and wood resins can enhance our physical and emotional well-being, according to some researchers. Holistic healers often use *aromatherapy* to ease ailments such as anxiety, depression, and breathing problems. The plant oils may be inhaled, massaged into the skin, or added to bath water. For the best effects, be sure to use *essential oils*—pure plant oils that are volatile and aromatic.

- Cedar: Speeds healing, purifies, and enhances your spiritual connection.

- Eucalyptus: Clears congestion and improves concentration.

- Juniper Berry: Calms the emotions, enhances healing, and fosters a sense of love and protection.

- Lavender: Puts the body and spirit at ease, and evokes deep serenity.

- Orange: Restores strength and uplifts the spirit.

- Patchouli: Stimulates the senses and restores tired muscles.

- Peppermint: Clears the mind; stimulates and refreshes.

- Pine: Invites a deep sense of relaxation, purifies, and promotes healing.

- Rosemary: Purifies, heals, refreshes sore muscles, and encourages loving protection.

- Sage: Regulates the central nervous system, eases night sweats, soothes sore throats, and promotes healing and protection.

- Sandalwood: Enhances sexuality, healing, and spirituality.

- Thyme: Encourages love, eases insomnia, and soothes bronchial infections.

- Verbena: Lowers blood pressure and eases stress.

- Ylang-Ylang: Ignites passion and desire, heightens joy, and creates an atmosphere for romance.

OPPOSITE

In an open living area, a beautifully crafted "bed box" creates a private space for sleep or relaxation. A shallow cabinet at the foot of the bed stores personal items.

"For the sense of smell, almost more than any other, has the power to recall memories and it is a pity that we use it so little."

Rachel Carson (1907–1964), U.S. biologist and author

HEALTHY SPACES FOR CHILDREN

"Childhood is measured out by sounds and smells..."

**John Betjeman (1906–1984),
British poet**

Designing spaces for the very young is both thrilling and frightening. Children are sensitive to their surroundings and much more vulnerable than adults to toxins, allergens, and other environmental hazards. Moreover, the rooms children inhabit shape their intellectual and emotional well-being in more ways that we can calculate. Long after they are grown, children hold fast to memories of the places where they slept and played.

The healthiest environment will be cozy and private yet not isolated from the bustle of family activities. Young children are likely to feel uneasy if their bedrooms are on a different floor or a separate wing from their parents. For many children, sharing a bedroom with a brother or sister is comforting, and also encourages a spirit of cooperation. However, every child needs private space to dream and pursue individual interests. When two or more children must be placed in a single room, a sliding screen or curtain will help each maintain a sense of ownership.

Keep in mind that a small child will not share your concept of space or distance. A room that an adult perceives as cramped may feel safe and reassuring to a four-year-old. Instead of a single large room, consider creating several child-friendly areas throughout the house. Even a tiny pantry can become an enchanted retreat for quiet play or an afternoon nap.

As children mature, their needs and interests undergo rapid evolution. Every few years they will want to reinvent the spaces they claim as their own. If you encourage the child to participate in design decisions, creating and recreating these rooms will become an important journey of self-discovery.

"Do not confine your children to
your own learning, for they were
born in another time."

Chinese proverb

Freedom from Chemicals...

Ideally, the entire home will be free of synthetics and manufactured materials that contain toxic chemicals. This goal takes on added urgency when designing rooms for children. Infants do not have fully developed immune, reproductive, or nervous systems. A baby's liver and kidneys cannot effectively flush harmful substances from the body. While an adult may be unaffected by exposure to a toxin such as lead, the infant will suffer serious impairment.

As children move from infancy to adolescence, their tissues and organs quickly grow and develop. Children breathe more rapidly and inhale more toxins per pound of body weight. When exposed to air pollution, children are much more likely than adults to suffer bronchitis, pneumonia, ear infections, and asthma.

To add to these risks, children's young days are spent crawling, playing, and sitting on the floor where dust and pollens collect. Naturally curious, children want to touch and taste the world around them. They require healthy spaces that encourage their need to explore while protecting them from harm.

As you plan special places for children, take a careful inventory and remove any items that contain volatile organic compounds (VOCs) (see page 84). Also, remove heavy carpeting and bedding that can collect dust or harbor mold.

OPPOSITE

Seafoam green creates a soothing atmosphere for infants. The cribs are placed at a safe distance from shelves, lamps, and window blinds.

If Your Child Has Allergies...

- Avoid wall-to-wall carpeting.

- Keep pets away from sleeping areas.

- Choose easy-to-clean toys made of wood or metal.

- Use roller shades instead of curtains.

- Store toys in a cabinet or closed chest.

What is a *Volatile Organic Compound?*

Most synthetic products manufactured during the past fifty years contain volatile substances that quickly evaporate, creating vapors that may be toxic. These gas-producing substances, called volatile organic compounds, or VOCs, are a major cause of air pollution inside the home.

Literally hundreds of different chemicals contained in VOCs are found in plywood, particleboard, paints, adhesives, synthetic fabrics, and cleaning products. Listed below are just three of the most common and most harmful. Fortunately, these fumes do dissipate over time. To minimize toxins, choose older furnishings and carpeting, or let new products air out before introducing them into the home. Best yet, choose all-natural materials that have not been treated with chemicals.

Formaldehyde

You can't see it, but formaldehyde emitting from paints, pressed wood furnishings, carpeting, and some forms of insulation will cause headaches, eye irritations, breathing difficulties, and hives and other allergies. Formaldehyde exposure may also trigger asthma in children.

Benzene

Used in the production of plastics, detergents, and petroleum-based fuels, high levels of benzene exposure cause leukemia, lymphoma, and other cancers. Chronic low-level exposure may result in headaches, drowsiness, depression, and loss of appetite.

Trichloroethylene

Used in dry cleaning and textile processing, trichloroethylene is associated with liver cancer. Adhesives, lubricants, paints, varnishes, and rubber materials may also contain trace amounts of this toxic, colorless chemical.

OPPOSITE

Low shelves, wicker baskets, and sliding trundle boxes supply quick and easy storage for games and small toys. Warm, earthy terra-cotta, salmon, and peach tones help a child feel secure.

"There is always one moment
in childhood when the door
opens and lets the future in."

Graham Greene (1904–1991), *The Power and the Glory*

OPPOSITE

Nontoxic water-based paint in deep green and blue help coordinate furnishings and create an environment that soothes and reassures. A rush mat softens sound on the solid oak floor.

FLOORS

Most synthetic carpeting emits formaldehyde and other VOCs that are especially harmful to children. Carpeting also traps dust and mold that will aggravate allergies in some children. Instead of wall-to-wall-carpeting, lay easy-to-wash natural fiber area rugs on a wood floor coated with a low-VOC urethane or paint. Natural linoleum or cork floors are also good options so long as they have been installed with low-VOC adhesives.

FURNISHINGS AND WOODWORK

It is always best to avoid items made of particleboard and other composition wood products manufactured with formaldehyde and other VOCs. Also, beware of painted surfaces. Prior to 1978, many paints contained lead, a toxic mineral associated with attention deficits, decreased IQ scores, learning disabilities, and hyperactivity in children. Toddlers who chew on painted toys or window ledges can ingest fatal doses of lead-laden paint. Paint dust collecting on windowsills will be inhaled by anyone in the area. To test the lead content in your home, use a simple kit available from most hardware stores. Furnishings and woodwork coated with lead-based paint should be removed from the area. Walls may be replastered or thoroughly coated with a water-based, low-VOC lead paint sealant.

BEDDING

The most comfortable and least toxic fabrics are pure cotton. Be wary of bed linens labeled as permanent press, wrinkle-resistant, anti-static, water-repellant, or stain-repellent. They have been treated with chemicals that may prove irritating or harmful. To be safe, wash and dry bedding three times before bringing it into the child's room. Avoid old mattresses; they are likely to contain mold and dust mites.

CLEANING SOLUTIONS

Fragrances and chemicals in commercial detergents can irritate children's skin, eyes, nose, and throat. As much as possible, use cleaning products that do not have chemical additives. Avoid chlorine bleach, fabric softeners, anti-cling solutions, and stain-removing solvents. Also, do not dry clean children's clothes or bedding; the process creates fumes that will linger for at least a week. Instead of commercial cleaners, use natural alternatives such as lemon juice, vinegar, salt, and bicarbonate of soda. Also, nonperfumed soap, borax, and washing soda are gentler than most detergents.

Human-centered Spaces...

Children are often fascinated by technological wonders. Unchecked, bedrooms and play areas can become collecting grounds for computers, televisions, video games, and a proliferation of toys that hum, buzz, and beep. Even an infant's room may accumulate a clutter of gadgetry as parents add clocks, radios, and baby monitors.

We do not yet know to what extent the low-frequency electromagnetic waves from electrical devices affect the health of developing children. While it is not realistic to ban technology from a twenty-first-century home, caring designers will want to think carefully about how much equipment is placed in sleeping areas. In addition to the electromagnetic waves they emit, computers, televisions, stereos, and cell phones can breed isolation. For the psychological as well as the physical health of the child, electronic toys and tools are best located in central living areas. As an added protection against electromagnetic waves, avoid furniture made of metal and check the placement of the child's bed. A large appliance such as a refrigerator on the other side of the wall will create a magnetic field.

When it is free from the silent energies radiating from electrical equipment, the child's room becomes a nurturing, human-centered place for rest, creative play, and quiet reflection.

"There is no doubt that for most of us, the childhood dwelling and its environs is the place of first getting in touch with who we are as distinct personalities."

Clare Cooper Marcus, *House as a Mirror of Self*

Safety Checklist

- Place cribs away from shelves, lamps, and cords.

- Remove pillows from cribs.

- Use beds with safety rails for toddlers.

- Remove any small object a child could choke on.

- Place lamps and shelves where they cannot be easily toppled.

- Make sure the pull cords on window blinds are not tied in a loop.

- Avoid long curtains.

- Avoid long, dangling electrical cords.

- Install childproof electrical sockets or outlet covers.

- Avoid track lighting and other open light fixtures.

- Install a non-ionizing smoke detector.

- Remove locks from doors.

- Keep halls and stairways well lit; place nightlights around the house.

ABOVE

Televisions and video games are best located away from sleeping areas. In this cheerful basement playroom, the electronics are tucked inside a cabinet with doors.

TOP LEFT

Long after they are grown, children will remember the colors used in their special rooms. For playrooms, create a fun mixture using the child's favorite hues.

BOTTOM LEFT

In the child's eye, furniture is not merely utilitarian; it enters the imagination and becomes an important part of creative play.

Make Room for Learning

- Stimulate your baby's senses with colorful mobiles and moving toys.

- Provide toys that let children swing, rock, and spin.

- Coat a wall area with chalkboard paint and supply plenty of colored chalk.

- Help children develop reasoning skills with puzzles and multi-colored geometric building blocks.

- Create an artist's corner with an ample supply of crayons, markers, paints, and clay.

- Inspire an interest in nature through aquariums, terrariums, and insect farms.

- Stimulate the imagination with fanciful wall murals and ceiling art.

- Use numbers and the alphabet in colorful graphic designs.

- Rearrange toys often to keep them fresh and exciting.

- Involve your children in decorating decisions as much as possible.

An Aura of Calm...

The successful children's space will stimulate the senses but not overwhelm them. Even when the child is in the midst of play and toys are scattered across the floor, an aura of order and calm will prevail so long as the room is designed for flexibility and ease. Provide rolling bins to stow toys under beds and tables. Build easy-to-reach cabinets under window seats. Supply playful containers that will entice children to pick up puzzle pieces and small toy parts.

To minimize the chance of accidents, make sure to choose age-appropriate furnishings. Children feel more secure and are less likely to fall when chairs, tables, and dressers are scaled to their size. Place drawers and shelves in easy reach. Use braces or anchors to firmly secure larger furniture to the wall. Avoid lamps that can be easily toppled.

Children are highly responsive to the emotional resonance of color and light. As adults, most of us have forgotten the important role that furniture plays in the imagination of a young child. A chair is not merely an object for sitting on: It is a tree, a castle, a boat, a space ship. By supplying chairs, stools, and tables in a variety of sizes, shapes, and colors, you encourage creativity.

A child who loves pink may crave its soothing properties. A child who has been depressed may feel more cheerful when surrounded by vivid greens. Ask your children what colors they like, and also observe behavior. Children may not always be able to express their tastes, but they will reveal their responses through body language and facial expressions. For playrooms, choose stimulating contrasts of bold primary colors: lemon yellow, fire engine red, bright blue. For sleeping or study areas, move toward softer shades of blue or green, or calming shades of peach, terra-cotta, salmon, or lavender.

Before repainting an entire room, try the color in one area and pay close attention to the child's response. The best colors are those that help the child feel happy, protected, and loved.

HEALTHY WORKPLACES

Home workplaces are as varied as the types of activities that take place there. An attic flooded with sunlight can be the ideal setting for a painter's studio, while a cozy kitchen corner may be all that's needed for household book-keeping. Large or small, secluded or in the midst of activity, these spaces are important to our well-being because they allow us to integrate work with family life. Moreover, a workplace that supplements or replaces an office outside the home helps reduce traffic, pollution, and other drains on the environment.

Regardless of its size and location in the house, the healthy workplace is designed to enhance concentration and foster creativity. If fume-producing inks or paints are required, attention is paid to safe storage and thorough ventilation. If the room contains computers, fax machines, and other techno-logical equipment, special care is taken to reduce the effects of electromag-netic currents. While striving for productivity, the user also takes into account the social and ecological impact of activities that take place here. Even a streamlined office filled with high-tech equipment will express caring and appreciation for nature.

Creating an area for productive work begins by minimizing distractions. Desktop clutter screaming for attention will sap your energy and disrupt your concentration. To bring order to the workspace, look for storage that has closing doors. Use an armoire or a rolltop desk to tuck files and work equipment out of sight when they are not needed. Hide heavy office machines behind a folding screen. Use pegboards to hang scissors and other tools, and bulletin boards to organize notes and business cards. Put pens in ceramic vases and paperclips in apothecary drawers. Place items you use most frequently beside your chair, or use a rolling cart so you can easily move supplies around the room.

Also pay close attention to the emotional impact of color, lighting, and furniture arrangements. *Feng shui* and *vástu shástra* offer numerous sugges-tions on where to place the desk or worktable to enhance feelings of confi-dence and security. Even if you choose not to closely follow the ancient laws, you may find that you can concentrate better when you are seated with an easy view of the doorway.

"Where I make a living, there is my home."

Somali proverb

OPPOSITE

A stone floor and potted plants pull the out-doors into a narrow studio. Placing the drafting table to face windows helps create a sense of spaciousness.

HEALTHY SEATING

Poor posture will cause fatigue and undermine your ability to think clearly or work productively. Choose a desk chair that supports your spine and allows you to sit at an appropriate height. With knees slightly bent, your feet should rest flat on the floor. With elbows bent at right angles, your hands should rest comfortably on the tabletop. A chair that swivels and glides easily over the floor will also enhance your comfort and efficiency.

HEALTHY LIGHTING

Warm natural sunshine combined with focused task lighting will prevent eye-strain and headaches. If the workplace is equipped with a computer, make sure that the monitor does not directly face a window or other light source. Also consider covering the monitor with a filter to reduce glare and sharpen the image.

Feng Shui for the Work Space

- Choose a large wooden desk.

- Place the desk cater-corner to the doorway.

- Arrange seating so it does not face a wall.

- Eliminate clutter.

- Use plants with rounded leaves to soften sharp corners.

- Beware of stairs that face the entrance; they will drain your workspace of energy.

- Avoid placing machines near the doorway.

- Know your directions. To foster tranquility, place a peace lily in the northern corner.

"Work is half of health."

Swedish proverb

FRESH AIR

Many home workplaces contain equipment and materials that have unusually high toxicity. Budget-priced office furniture is often made of pressboard, plastics, and other formaldehyde-emitting substances. Photocopiers and laser printers create sharp, headache-inducing fumes. Inks, markers, artist paints, glues, and even bleached paper contribute to the chemical cocktail. To compound the problem, a workplace located in a basement or small back bedroom may not receive enough fresh air ventilation.

Opening a window may be the most important step you can take to improve air quality in the home office or workshop. Also, consider adding a fan for air circulation and a freestanding HEPA air filter to help remove impurities. If possible, place the photocopy machine and laser printer in a ventilated area outside the room. Use unbleached recycled paper and nontoxic art supplies, and be sure to store paints and inks in tightly sealed containers. Finally, to freshen the air, give the room a healthy dose of green: Hang wispy spider plants at the window and sit cascading English ivy in darker corners.

OPPOSITE

The ergonomic office chair need not look institutional. This one is tall enough to support the head and shoulders. It also swivels and glides easily under the desk.

ABOVE

Floor-to-ceiling shelves help keep the work area organized and clutter-free. A gliding wooden ladder allows easy access to upper shelves.

Protect Yourself from Electromagnetic Radiation

- Make sure electrical connections are well grounded.

- Upgrade to a low radiation TCO-certified monitor or a flat-panel LCD monitor.

- Shield your existing monitor with a grounded, radiation-reducing glare guard.

- Use a battery-operated portable computer.

- Use incandescent lighting; avoid fluorescents.

- Avoid using cellular phones.

- Avoid unnecessary electrical devices. Sharpen pencils manually.

- Place seating away from copy machines and other heavy equipment.

- Place surge protectors away from your feet.

"Work is good provided you do not forget to live."

Bantu proverb

HEALTHY HARDWARE

No one knows to what extent our health is affected by the electromagnetic radiation emitted by computers and other office equipment. Although research is inconclusive, the health-minded designer will want to err on the side of caution and move nonessential machines out of the immediate area. If you must work at a computer, consider placing the peripheral equipment inside a closet or cabinet. Arrange the desk so that you do not sit directly over a surge protector or electrical cords. And, most importantly, if you have not done so already, upgrade to equipment that meets "TCO" (The Swedish Confederation of Professional Employees) guidelines. TCO is a strict list of standards applied worldwide to computer displays, keyboards, hard drives, printers, copiers, and mobile phones. About half of all computer monitors manufactured today bear the TCO-approved label.

By definition, TCO-approved equipment has low emissions of electromagnetic radiation, and also conserves energy by incorporating rest modes and other power-saving strategies. In addition, the equipment must meet standards for ease of use, providing nonglare monitors that minimize eyestrain.

OPPOSITE

Natural wood, wicker, earthen pottery, and fresh flowers soften the effects of essential electronic equipment in a home office. A clutter-free table at the center of the room provides a serene workspace away from the computer.

The Earth-Friendly Workspace

Whether the workplace is a high-tech office with TCO-approved equipment or a back-to-basics studio with an easel and a stool, waste is inevitable. Machinery and bright task lighting hog energy, and a busy worker is likely to discard reams of paper, most of which will end up in landfills. Added to this is the pollution caused by outdated computers, printers, and fax machines that cannot be recycled.

For an earth-friendly workspace, choose energy-efficient equipment and make sure to turn it off when it's not in use. As much as possible, donate outdated equipment and tools to schools, churches, libraries, or civic organizations. Many communities have a recycling coordinator who can suggest outlets for throwaways.

Practice conservation by eliminating bleached virgin paper. Recycled paper for correspondence or artwork may be purchased in virtually any size or weight. Also consider treeless paper. Hemp, kenaf, and other pulps are chlorine- and acid-free; papers manufactured from these materials do not spew dioxin and other pollutants into the environment.

"Work is the source of all good."

Thai proverb

OPPOSITE

Empty space in a stairway landing can be transformed into an airy work center with built-in shelves. Here, a white-on-white palette captures the light and enhances concentration.

Reduce Office Waste

- Consider buying used equipment.

- Seek equipment made of recycled materials.

- Buy equipment with energy-saving standby features.

- Avoid unnecessary printouts; do editing on-screen.

- Network home computers to share printers and other equipment.

- Send e-mails instead of letters.

- Use the back of discarded papers for notes and drafts.

- Use recycled paper products.

- Supply a bin for recycling waste paper.

- Reuse file folders and envelopes.

- Recycle printer cartridges.

- Turn off lights and equipment when not in use.

- Donate outdated equipment, or recycle it.

"When you discover your mission, you will feel its demand. It will fill you with enthusiasm and a burning desire to get to work on it."

W. Clement Stone, U.S. businessman and philanthropist

Seashells, flowers, and other details that speak to the soul act as powerful psychic cues, providing encouragement and inspiration.

Safety Checklist

- Use three-prong electrical outlets; they are grounded for safety.

- Never remove the third prong of a three-prong plug.

- Avoid using extension cords. If cords are necessary, unplug them when they are not in use.

- Never run electrical cords under carpets or across areas where you will walk.

- Check your main electrical panel. Add extra circuits if you need to plug in more than 1,500 watts.

- Unplug electrical equipment during lightning storms.

- Make sure light bulbs are the appropriate size for the fixture.

- Keep halogen lamps away from draperies.

- Turn off equipment if the cord feels hot or looks frayed.

Designed to Inspire...

Creativity does not come from tools or machines. The sharp metallic objects and cold plastics that dominate so many workspaces can seem overwhelming and forbidding unless they are softened with details that speak to the soul.

Be sure to incorporate elements of the world outside your windows. Place Gerbera Daisies in front of the printer; use a glittering chunk of quartz for a paperweight. Tuck electrical wires inside cable channels and wrap them with strips of moss-colored cotton.

As you plan the office or studio, take time to ask yourself what you hope to accomplish there and why the work is important. Even a desk set aside for managing the household budget becomes meaningful when you reflect on the future you are saving for. By considering the value of the work you do, you will be led to design decisions that will help humanize a room that might otherwise seem harsh and utilitarian.

Color can have a wonderful softening effect on any room. Begin with an energizing shade such as red and gently dim it to a muted mid-tone. To enhance concentration, move into darker hues. To encourage creativity, try a broad stroke of an unconventional color such as aqua.

Add artwork, photographs, and mementos that remind you of the importance and meaning of your work: A warm thank you letter from a client, an article about a successful person in your field, or a photograph of your family. Also display diplomas, awards, examples of completed projects, and other reminders of past successes. Rather than adding clutter, carefully selected details act as powerful psychic cues, providing encouragement and inspiration.

HEALING BATHS AND SPAS

"In the world there is nothing more submissive and weak than water. Yet for attacking that which is hard and strong nothing can surpass it."

**Lao-Tzu (c. 570 B.C.),
Chinese philosopher**

Water heals. Bubbling from fountains, burbling in atrium gardens, and steaming from deep wooden tubs, it has the power to ease pain, soothe the nerves, and refresh the spirit. Raw, dried herbs crumbled into hot water fill the air with healing fragrances. Mineral salts and crystals sprinkled into the bath draw out toxins and purify the skin. Misty steam cleanses the body and eases symptoms of colds, bronchitis, and allergies.

It's no wonder, then, that health-conscious designers are transforming the way bathrooms look and function. Gone are the cramped, strictly utilitarian rooms of days gone by. The healing home is likely to include a spacious body-care center with thoughtfully created facilities for cleansing and hydrotherapy. Combining up-to-the-minute technologies with ancient wisdom, these rooms may include Japanese-style soaking tubs or room-sized showers with powerful, deeply relaxing water jets. Exercise rooms, saunas, grooming centers, and even gardens become a part of these body-care complexes. Expanding the boundaries of the traditional bathroom, homeowners are also adding refrigerators, juice bars, and flat-screen televisions. An expansive bathing area may resemble a fully decorated living room in which the bathtub is only a part of the furnishings.

Yet, regardless of the amenities, the bathroom in the healthy home remains a quiet retreat: an escape from the noise, confusion, and electromagnetic energies of the modern world. Even in the midst of supreme comfort, the design of these rooms reflects an attitude of simplicity and restraint.

Honoring the ancient traditions of *feng shui* and *vástu shástra,* special care is given to the placement of mirrors and lighting. The healthy bathing area is well illuminated with soft, ambient light and thoughtfully arranged reflective surfaces. Sunlight shimmers through frosted glass windows and glistens on clean, smooth tile surfaces. If possible, the toilet is hidden in a separate room. However, even in the toilet area, beauty and serenity are guiding principles.

Feng Shui Wisdom

To protect yourself from negative *chi* in the bathroom:

- Keep the door closed and toilet seat cover down.

- Place a quartz or metallic crystal on the toilet tank.

- Grow tall plants to increase upward energy.

- Fix all leaks promptly.

- Use doors, curtains, screens, or crystals to separate the bathroom from sleeping and kitchen areas

Embracing Nature

Healing bathrooms are special places where we relish the sensations of our bodies. Yet, while celebrating the self, it is important to also express reverence for nature. Begin by choosing fixtures and details that are kind to the earth. Instead of fiberglass and other artificial compounds, choose marble, granite, or slate. As old as the earth, natural stone will long outlast factory-made imitations. Ceramics are also a good choice because they are made of the earth itself, and the glazes are made of minerals.

The water that cleanses and heals is a treasured resource, not to be squandered. Even if you do not wish to remodel your bathroom, you can conserve water by replacing older fixtures or adding simple devices to your existing fixtures. In a typical home, the toilet consumes 38 percent of the water used each day. Newer low-flush toilets use water conservatively while still providing enough to function smoothly. A "low flow" showerhead will reduce water flow by more than half, while retaining a satisfying, forceful spray. Aerators on the faucets will reduce the flow of water from 4 to 6 gallons per minute down to a mere $1/2$ gallon per minute. For added savings, install sink faucets that shut off automatically when the hand is withdrawn.

With its silky surfaces, water-inspired colors, uninhibited sunlight, and abundant foliage, the healthy bathroom blurs the boundaries between indoors and out. As you plan this important room, give yourself permission to experiment with unexpected combinations of stone and steel, light and shadow. Just as nature places a silky leaf on a rugged branch, you can combine luxury and rusticity. Set a shimmering stainless steel basin atop a granite counter. Rest an all-glass shower module on a rugged brick floor. Hang bamboo shelves on polished marble walls. And, when the sun sets, light naturally scented candles and watch their gentle light flicker across hand-painted porcelain tiles.

The Natural Bathroom

- Pave the floor in buffed marble, slate, stone, or brick.

- Surface the walls in terra-cotta tile.

- Furnish with bamboo chairs.

- Open windows to sunlit views.

- Hang seashells from shower walls.

- Place a bowl with goldfish on the counter.

- Grow peace lilies in ceramic jugs around the tub.

The Techno Bathroom

- Surface walls in brushed steel or gleaming black ceramic.

- Enclose bathing areas in frame-free glass doors.

- Hang glass shelves.

- Install stainless steel halogen spotlights.

- Keep piping exposed.

Turn bathing into a celebration of the spirit

- Light candles.

- Drape mirrors with English ivy.

- Play soft music.

- Use all-natural soaps and shampoos.

- Hang pictures that celebrate physical beauty.

- Sprinkle your bath water with dried sage, rose, or lavender.

- Dry with plush all-cotton towels.

ABOVE

Water can't puddle on a counter made of narrow wooden slats. Piping underneath the sink is exposed for easy cleaning and maintenance.

Designed for Comfort and Ease

Whether expansive or restrained, the healthy bathroom is designed for safety and ease of use. Design your bathroom to minimize the chance for slips and falls. Use nonslip stone or tile flooring and rush or cork mats. Install handrails beside the tub and along the shower walls. To prevent accidental burns, make sure that hot and cold faucets are clearly labeled. In older homes where the water pressure may be inconsistent, install thermostatic valves to keep water temperatures at safe levels. Also, check all outlets located near running water; they should be fitted with ground fault interrupter (GFI) circuits to prevent shocks.

Quick-dry wicker chairs add to the serenity of a bathing area. For comfortable seating, the sink may be wall-mounted with legroom below. Adjustable wall brackets will permit users to raise and lower the sink to the desired height. Small details play an important role. Install sleek lever faucet handles that turn on and off without causing arm and wrist strain. Consider the placement of the toilet paper roll: Users should never have to twist in odd positions to find it.

To minimize back, neck, and shoulder strain, bathing facilities are ideally designed according to ergonomic principles. Choose shower sprays that glide gently down to accommodate shorter bathers. Footsteps and seating benches will add to the safety and comfort of shower units. The most comfortable bathtubs are engineered to conform to the contours of the human body. Some recently designed tubs incorporate lumbar support to hold the bather in a comfortable position. Built-in head rests and arm rests make these ergonomic tubs feel more like recliners than plumbing fixtures.

For maximum relaxation, Whitewater Specialties Ltd. manufactures a new breed of "Smart Tub." Supple padding beneath a tough, nonporous "elastomeric" surface becomes pliant when the tub is filled with warm water. Surrounding the bather with womb-like comfort, the high-density foam core helps keep the water steamy and softly muffles sound.

OPPOSITE

All-cotton towels, all-natural shampoos, and plenty of natural sunlight help create a healthy bathing area.

Safety Checklist

- GFI (ground fault interrupter) electrical outlets

- Nonslip flooring

- Handrails

- Thermostatic valves

Bathing Basics

You do not have to install complicated facilities to enjoy the benefits of hydrotherapy. In rooms without whirlpools or saunas, try these simple therapies:

- Full Bath: To calm the nerves, soothe the sniffles, and ease urinary and bladder problems, sink shoulder deep in warm water.

- Sitz Bath: To ease menstrual problems or intestinal distress, sit hip deep in hot water followed by cold.

- Foot Bath: To improve circulation, lower blood pressure, and ease headaches and insomnia, soak your feet and calves in alternating hot and cold water.

- Vapor Bath: For colds or sinus problems, sit beneath a towel and inhale the vapors of very hot water scented with natural herbs or oils. To create a mini-spa, surround yourself with steaming pots.

"Aquadextrous, adj.: Possessing
the ability to turn the bathtub
faucet on and off with your toes."

Rich Hall, U.S. writer, *Sniglets*

"When you drink the water, remember the spring."

Chinese proverb

Fresh, Pure, and Clean

The warm waters that soothe muscles and calm the mind can also create health hazards if the moisture is not properly ventilated. Keeping bathing areas dry may be as simple as cracking open a window. Exhaust fans over the bath or shower and near the toilet help keep fresh air gently circulating. The toilet should have an insulated tank to minimize condensation.

To prevent the growth of mold and mildew, surface walls with easy-wipe brushed steel or pre-finished, factory-glazed ceramic tile. Hand-painted tiles with their quirky irregularities add charm and originality. Brilliantly colored mosaic tiles set in bold geometric or pictorial designs evoke the setting of an ancient Roman bath. Solid blocks or bands of bright color suggest energy and excitement. Tile grout, which can harbor mold or mildew spores, should be coated with a fume-free sealant. Toiletries become decorative objects when they are openly displayed on glass and metal shelves.

Prolonged exposure to moisture can cause fabrics to mildew. Liberate windows from bulky curtains. Frosted glass or tinted glass blocks will provide privacy in the bathing area. Extra towels should be stored away from the bathroom. Damp linens may be hung on heated rails in chrome, brass, or brushed nickel. On chilly days, the energy-efficient hydronic warmers will circulate hot water inside the hollow towel bars and help heat the entire room. An automatic shut-off will prevent accidental burns.

As in other rooms in the house, air purity is a primary concern. Throw away plastic shower curtains: They produce an unpleasant and potentially harmful chemical odor. The best shelving is made of solid wood, glass, wicker, or metal. Sink basins will become objets d'art in brushed stainless steel, clear glass, and virtuous china. For their purity and their moisture-resistance, iroko, merbau, and other hearty tropical woods are favored. Natural slate, blue stone, and brick are preferred to vinyl and other engineered compounds.

By mingling sleek glass and metals with the soft patina of wood and stone, you may create refreshing spaces that are remarkably easy to keep clean. Exposed piping becomes a part of the decor and facilitates cleaning and maintenance. Even in an older home rich in decorative detail, aspire to simplicity in the bathroom. Toilets with smooth, skirted pedestals and easy-clean glazings will help keep the room germ-free. A combination toilet and bidet from Toto of Japan offers the ultimate in sanitation by incorporating automatic controls. At the push of a button, it washes, dries, regulates the water temperature, and opens and closes the lid. There is no need for paper tissue.

To Prevent Mildew

- Open a window, or use a fan.

- Store extra towels away from bathing areas.

- Replace curtains with frosted glass.

- Use a dehumidifier.

- Install a heat lamp.

- Hang damp towels and bathmats on heated rails.

- Wipe shower walls after each use.

Filtered for Safety

When the ancient Greeks and Romans celebrated the healing properties of water, they bathed in hot springs bubbling up from the earth. Unfortunately, the water in our homes is not as clean or pure. Whether drawn from a municipal reservoir or a private well, the water is likely to contain trace amounts of minerals or bacteria. Lead piping in older homes can also add contamination.

The first step in assuring water purity is to hire a testing laboratory to conduct a thorough analysis. Impurities in drinking water may be removed by placing small filtration devices at the sink and faucets. However, if the bathing water is not filtered, lead, copper, and other minerals will be absorbed through the skin and into the blood stream. For this reason, it is wise to install a complete water filtration system for the entire household.

Whirlpool tubs with their powerful water jets are deeply relaxing, but some models may also become a source of impurities. If the tubs are not maintained properly, unsanitary sediment trapped in the piping can seep back into the bathing water. As a precaution, many homeowners are opting for pipeless whirlpool systems such as those manufactured by Sanijet. Other homeowners are replacing whirlpools altogether with easy-clean soaking tubs and eco-friendly shower systems.

For Pure Water...

Be sure to choose the filtration system that best meets your needs.

- *Carbon filter* systems remove radon, organic chemicals, and pesticides.

- *Reverse-osmosis* systems remove lead, salt, and other heavy metals.

- *KDF (kinetic degradation fluxation)* systems control bacteria and some heavy metals.

- *Distillation* systems remove salt, sediment, and heavy metals.

- *Sediment filter* systems remove sand, dirt, and other particles.

Take Your Toiletries from Nature

All-natural soap and personal care products are available from most health stores or via mail order. Or you may wish to make your own.

- Moisturizers and conditioners: Experiment with milk, yogurt, egg yolk, oatmeal, and olive or safflower oil.

- Aftershave: Use witch hazel.

- Toothpaste: Mix baking soda and salt. If desired, add fresh peppermint.

- Perfumes: Use essential oils to scent shampoo, bath oil, and cleaning products.

Natural Cleaning

- Toilet bowl: Create a sudsing cleanser with baking soda and vinegar, or combine borax with lemon juice.

- Tub and shower: Wipe with vinegar, then rub with baking soda on a damp cloth.

Hydrotherapy

Thanks to modern developments in tub and shower technologies, bathers can enjoy a variety of sophisticated hydrotherapies in the privacy of their homes. Sculpted to the body and equipped with massaging water jets and temperature controls, tubs take on every imaginable shape, from the traditional rectangle to rustic pondlike formations. Enclosed in glass, steel, or colorful mosaic tiles, showers may fit comfortably in a narrow corner or expand to fill an entire room.

THERMO-MASSAGE WHIRLPOOLS

Tubs that provide water massage have powerful air and water jets positioned to stimulate or relax the body's pressure points. These tubs may also have air injectors at the bottom to gently lift the bather on effervescent swirls of bubbles.

SOAKING TUBS

More and more health-conscious bathers are adopting the ancient Japanese tradition of washing before entering the tub. Designed for soaking rather than cleansing, the Japanese-style tub permits bathers to sit chin deep in steaming water. High-tech versions may include jet streams and other modern innovations, but in the truly authentic soaking tub, the only sound and motion comes from the gentle lapping of the water. Made of traditional white cedar, copper, or stainless steel, modern soaking tubs range from compact three-foot models to spa-sized with ample room for a bathing companion. Some models are equipped with an overflow pool; water spilling over the rim recirculates into the tub.

CHROMOTHERAPY TUBS

Designed by Kohler, this modernistic variation of the Japanese-style tub combines deep soaking with color therapy. Four LED (light emitting diodes) lights along the inner walls of the tub transmit eight healing hues. Pulsating in intensity, each color washes over the bather for eight seconds, and then fades into a new shade.

"Noble deeds and hot baths are the best cures for depression."

Dodie Smith (1896–1990), English dramatist

UNDERWATER MASSAGE

Any tub can become the setting for deeply relaxing underwater massage. The only equipment needed is a flexible hose with a spray nozzle and a speed coupler. Controlled by a switch or lever, the pressure of water jets sends probing heat to sore muscles and aching joints.

SAUNA

The traditional Scandinavian sauna is a pine-walled cabin heated to very high temperatures. Water poured over hot stones quickly evaporates and the air remains extremely dry. Modern homeowners may purchase freestanding sauna units with remote controls to regulate the heat. A few minutes in these hot, arid enclosures produces heavy perspiration, widening the pores and enhancing antibodies against colds and infections. A bracing shower after each session sloughs off sweat and worldly worries.

ABOVE

Frosted glass windows cast a soothing glow on the tranquil waters of an ultra-deep tub. A drip tray catches water cascading over the rim.

Healing Steam...Soothing Scents

STEAM ENCLOSURES

Unlike a traditional Scandinavian sauna, a steam room is a moist environment. Inspired by the Turkish baths of antiquity, the enclosure is warmed to humid temperatures of 40°C to 50°C (104°F to 122°F). The moist, gentle warmth is both relaxing and revitalizing. The cloudy mists of vapor bring welcome relief from the symptoms of asthma, hay fever, and colds.

AROMATHERAPY

Added to modular steam enclosures or smaller steam-producing units, fragrant natural oils create healing vapors that are inhaled and also absorbed through the skin. To ease stress and rejuvenate the spirit, bask in the aroma of verbena or ylang-ylang. Choose eucalyptus to improve breathing and patchouli to stimulate the senses (see *Healing Fragrances,* page 78).

VERTICAL SPAS

Although they entice with promises of luxury, whirlpools and soaking tubs are often not the first choice for conservation-minded homeowners. Tubs require many gallons of water to fill, and whirlpool jets need extra maintenance. Where space is limited, designers recommend vertical spa modules. Resembling "sci-fi" space vessels, sleek European models are equipped with multiple showerheads, computerized temperature controls, and even built-in sound systems. Strategically placed water jets provide the same type of hydro massage found in whirlpools—and place less demand on natural resources.

WETROOMS

Expanding to fill an entire room, the shower becomes a steamy rainforest with a drain at the center. Oversized showerheads on opposing walls invite two or more people to share the space. The room may include a sink, a toilet, or soul-pleasing amenities such as tropical foliage, mosaic tile murals, or brightly colored children's squirt toys.

ABOVE

Mossy green hues pull nature into a tile-lined bathing area. The shell-studded chandelier is a playful tribute to the ocean. Insulating honeycomb shades offer warmth and privacy.

Bathroom Themes

In the healthy home, the bathing areas nurture both body and spirit.

- Home Gym: Add a treadmill, stationary bike, weight machine, and other exercise equipment.

- Grooming Center: Combine a console sink with comfortable seating and a well-lit magnifying mirror.

- Art Gallery: Water-resistant artifacts such as sculpture and stained glass add a spiritual dimension.

- Garden: Recreate Eden with moisture-loving tropical plants.

- Aquarium: Bathe with brightly colored tropical fish, displayed in tanks.

SACRED SPACES

A walled garden with water trickling past a rain-worn Buddha…a bedroom alcove draped with hand-woven tapestries…a profoundly silent, subterranean room illuminated by candles. Peaceful sanctuaries like these are not mere luxuries. Whether or not we practice an organized religion, we all require calm and privacy to reflect on our lives and affirm our connection with the universe.

Over the past decade, dozens of research studies have shown that private meditation reduces depression and anxiety, enhances physical well-being, and increases longevity. A home sanctuary is a fundamental part of any dwelling concerned with body and spirit. Like the Hindu *puja* room, it is a fortress of purity and a center of spiritual energy. Like the *zendo* of Zen Buddhist tradition, it provides a peaceful, supremely quiet environment for meditation. Regardless of the size and design of the room, it is free from the noise and distractions that crowd our everyday lives.

Within these guidelines, your home sanctuary may take on many roles. You may use this space to honor a divinity or simply to relax and let go of routine worries. You may spend your time reading, listening to music, singing, playing an instrument, chanting, meditating, or writing.

Although designed for solitude, the room may also provide a comforting setting for group prayer and intimate conversations with family and friends. The sanctity of the room is protected so long as you use it only for activities that nourish the soul. Televisions, telephones, computers, and other worldly objects have no place here. Any reminders of daily concerns are left outside the door. Place a *mandala,* blossoming gardenia, or sacred symbol at the threshold to protect the boundaries of your sacred space. If you use this space regularly, at the same time each day, the healing practices of meditation will soothe your mind, comfort your body, and embrace the world with loving energy.

"Better to do a kindness near home than go far away to burn incense."

Chinese proverb

Find Your Sacred Space

No home is too small to house a meditation room. Seek an area that is set aside from the bustle of family life. Any of these areas will do:

- An unfinished attic with vaulting rafters

- A walk-in closet with cotton pillows on the floor

- A bedroom corner behind hanging beads or a branching Ficus tree

- A cellar room painted cleansing white

- An outdoor gazebo or arbour draped with morning glory

- A bathing area where warm, flowing waters stir primordial memories

Begin with Emptiness...

Your sacred space will be defined by the activities that take place there. Begin with a thorough cleaning of the area. Remove any items that contain unnatural and potentially toxic elements. By cleansing the room, you help to empty your mind. You may wish to empty the room entirely, and then add only those items that are necessary and meaningful. Consult with each person who will be using the room; avoid introducing any elements that another might find distracting or discomforting.

By preparing the space slowly and thoughtfully, you help to establish an atmosphere of calm reflection. You may want to say a prayer or do a ritual blessing according to the traditions of your faith. As part of the process, also bless each object that is brought into the room.

ICONS

Bring to your sanctuary images that have special resonance for you. Steeped in meaning, crosses, menorahs, Buddha carvings, *Ganesh* figures, and other icons provide grace and symmetry. Yin-yang patterns and other mystical designs combine beauty with profound concepts. If your household practices more than one faith, design the sacred space to reflect the intricate tapestry of your family.

OPPOSITE

Aqua hues suggest deep waters in this serene meditation area. Candles, rocks, and water lilies nestle in the quiet pond.

RIGHT

To blur the boundaries between indoors and out, choose fabrics that softly echo the colors and patterns of nature.

"Some keep the Sabbath going
to Church—
I keep it, staying at Home—
With a Bobolink for a Chorister—
And an Orchard, for a Dome."

Emily Dickinson (1830–1886), U.S. poet

VISUAL ART

Spirituality is not a prescribed system of beliefs, but an energy that is intrinsic with our physical, emotional, and intellectual beings. For many of us, the highest form of worship and celebration is through secular art. Display paintings and sculptures that reflect your most deeply cherished ideals. An impressionistic landscape may evoke thoughts of love and serenity. An abstract work may soothe and inspire through the interplay of color, pattern, and texture.

Your sacred space may also be a place to create art, provided that the creative act is done prayerfully rather than through vanity or ambition. Your own artwork displayed in this room becomes a way to connect with your higher self.

Create a
Quiet Space

- Mask outside noises with wind chimes and other soothing sounds.

- Play recordings of forest sounds or birdcalls.

- Install an indoor water fountain.

- Bring in tall, leafy plants to help muffle noise.

- If allergies are not a concern, use heavy drapes, soft pillows, plush carpeting, and fabric wall hangings to absorb sound.

MEMENTOS

Use the sacred space to honor your ancestors and to cherish family memories. Display antique photographs and letters from grandparents. Hang children's artwork, or invite your children to paint a brilliantly colored wall mural. Create a detailed family tree with loving facts about each person listed. Or, inscribe the name of an honored ancestor on a traditional Japanese *ihai* made of shimmering black lacquer.

HANDICRAFTS

You may also choose to use this space to honor the family of humankind. Gather together handicrafts from many cultures. Discover the thrilling juxtaposition of color and texture when you set Mexican pottery on persimmon-bright Thai silk. Mingle rough-hewn woodcarvings with polished mahogany, hammered tin with etched brass, raw clay with glazed porcelain.

BOOKS

Books in beautiful bindings provide comfort and inspiration. On a small easel or a traditional *tatimi* table, display a family Bible, a copy of the Koran, the sayings of Buddha, or writings from prophets and sages. Or choose a volume of poetry, a collection of essays, a meditation book, or a novel that evokes gratitude and joy. Enrich this collection with your own writings. Keep bound journals of your meditations along with a plentiful supply of fine-tipped pens and richly textured recycled paper.

MUSIC

Music is food for the soul. Fill your sacred space with the sounds of Sibelius or Pachelbel. Listen to great choral works, exquisite notes of the Japanese *koto,* or the haunting rhythms of African drums. Play tapes or CDs of sounds that inspire you, or create your own music. Discover the joy of music making through singing, chanting, drumming, strumming, ringing bells, or blowing a bamboo flute. Also be sure to introduce the timeless sounds of nature. Play recordings of whale songs and falling rain. Open a window to let in the symphony of birds and the rustle of leaves.

OPPOSITE

Moving water brings healthy chi *to a serene courtyard sanctuary. Tall flowering plants lift the spirit.*

"My job as a minister is not only to make heaven my home, but to make my home on earth sheer heaven."

Joseph Losery, U.S. minister and civil rights leader

> "Sitting quietly, doing nothing, spring comes and the grass grows by itself."

Zen proverb

SILENCE

Your sacred space may not be the best place for sophisticated stereo equipment. Weigh your desire to listen to meaningful recordings against the disadvantages of introducing electronic devices into the spiritual heart of your home. Even a small tape player will emit electromagnetic waves that may subtly interfere with your meditative state. Consider the value of silence. Your sacred room may be the only still place in a home that hums with human energy and vibrates with the sounds of televisions, radios, and whirring appliances. Use this silence to listen to your breathing and to sink deep inside yourself. Protect the silence. Cover walls and floors with natural cork tiles, plush carpets made of pure wool, or other materials which will absorb distracting noise from the outside world.

ILLUMINATION

Just as silence can help you hear your inner wisdom, darkness may light your journey. Turn off overhead fixtures. A darkened room lets you focus on scents, sounds, and tactile sensations. You may find yourself seeing more clearly when you cannot see at all. To add a soothing glow, place lighted candles in colorful ceramic dishes. A sacred room with a fireplace offers the opportunity to worship as our ancestors did, contemplating flickering flames and glowing embers. Artificial logs made of wax and compressed sawdust may be preferable to hardwood, because they produce less carbon monoxide.

For reading and other activities that require task lighting, supply a lamp with a shade made of stained glass or natural handmade paper pressed with leaves and flowers. During the day, open blinds and let natural sunshine filter through cotton gauze or rattan shades. A round skylight, soft uplighting in corners, or gentle illumination around a treasured artifact will add to the ethereal atmosphere in the room.

SENSUAL DETAILS

Even if your spiritual space is steeped in darkness and silence, it need not be a place of sensory deprivation. Spiritual awakening will bring a heightened awareness of touch, aroma, and taste. Nourish your physical self with details that comfort and delight. Cover pillows with brushed cotton. Nestle water-worn stones in a china bowl. Sprinkle the air with lilac, lavender, sage, and other mood-enhancing fragrances. Sip spiced tea or fresh orange juice from a crystal cup.

The *Zendo*

In the tradition of Zen Buddhism, the *zendo* is a room or hall devoted to *zazen* and other zen practices. Whether located in a monastery or a private home, the *zendo* provides a serene atmosphere for meditation.

- The room should be free of music, televisions, and other distractions.

- Sparsely furnished, the *zendo* may contain prayer mats, wooden benches, and a *butsudan,* or altar.

- A traditional Japanese *butsudan* is a large cabinet made of black lacquer. It may hold an incense burner, fresh flowers, and tablets inscribed with the names of family ancestors.

Reverence for Nature

Only by connecting with earth can we discover our spirit. Imbue your sacred space with life energy. If the room is blessed with sunlight, bring in pots of blossoming blue hyacinth, symbolizing the spirit and eternal life. Fill clear glass vases with purple iris and large white lilies. Float fragrant lotus blossoms in a bowl. Be sure to change the water every day, and promptly remove any plant that is wilted; dying vegetation will sap essential life energy from the room. Speak to your plants and tend to them lovingly. In this way you will also nourish your soul.

Invite pets into the room. The rhythmic motion and tactile pleasure of stroking warm fur will help wash away troubling thoughts. Animals also represent our guides to the spiritual plane. By exploring our connection with our pets, we open ourselves to our own repressed animal natures and discover important aspects of our souls. If you do not have a pet, you may want to bring in a carving or painting depicting animal life. Even a stuffed toy will recall loving childhood moments and stir feelings of tenderness.

For their beauty, motion, and potent symbolism, birds and fish can be important presences in a sacred space. Representing the soul, canaries and finches will fill the room with song and color. If the area is secure, open the doors to their cages and let them try their wings. Tropical fish suggest deep thought and remind us of our own primordial beginnings. Place an aquarium on a low table where you can comfortably watch the hypnotic fluid movement and iridescent color.

Water itself is our very essence. A miniature fountain will fill your room with the comforting sound of water trickling over rocks. A meditation area in the bath or spa will allow you to contemplate your soul while floating in womb-like warmth. For their complex textures, subtle hues, and timeless qualities, shells and rocks make meaningful additions to your indoor waterscape.

OPPOSITE

A bubbling bath with garden views becomes a quiet place to celebrate both body and spirit. The rich hues and warm texture of terra-cotta tile reaffirm earthly connections.

"A rock pile ceases to be a rock pile the moment a single man contemplates it, bearing within him the image of a cathedral."

Antoine de Saint-Exupery (1900–1944), French writer, philosopher

The *Puja* Room

Love and joy come to Hindu families who rise before dawn and honor divinity through *puja,* or worship. Beautifully decorated to resemble a small temple, the *puja* room is a sacred sanctuary located in the northeast corner of the home.

- The room should be well illumi-nated and draft-free.

- Worshipers must face east.

- The altar may be close to the floor, where worshippers are seated.

- Any image representing the deity must not face south.

- The room must never be used for sleeping.

Furnishings that Lift Your Spirit

Eschewing vanity and excess, the home sanctuary speaks to the soul. Beyond the special items you bring to inspire a prayerful state, you will need very little in the way of furnishings. An antique rocking chair will encourage contemplation through rhythmic motion. A cushion on the floor will allow you to practice Buddhist, Zen, yoga, or transcendental traditions. Or you may choose furnishings that are ergonomically designed for yoga and other varieties of meditation.

PRAYER MATS

A woolen carpet, a folded blanket, or a simple mat may offer sufficient padding for legs, knees, ankles, and feet. Although not as soft, a *tatami* mat made of bamboo or rice straw offers a pleasing, natural texture. A traditional *zabuton* seating pad offers more cushioning. The pad may be stuffed with cotton batting or organic fillings that create soothing swishing sounds as they move and shift shapes.

PILLOWS

A plump pillow will help prevent cramped legs and feet and also will provide enough height for sitting at a small table. Treat yourself to a traditional round meditation pillow (or *zafu*) that has been formed into a cozy crescent shape.

MEDITATION CHAIRS

Hugging the floor, a chair designed for meditation supports your back while giving you freedom to assume traditional postures. Some sleek contemporary versions have legs that unfold so that you can adjust the height as needed.

TABLES

A low table or a simple wooden pedestal will give you just enough space on which to display a treasured sculpture or set a pot of steaming tea. If you plan to use your sacred space for reading, studying, or journaling, provide a small desk with pens or pencils in ceramic jars. Transform an antique occasional table into a shrine or altar, and use a painted wood trunk to hold scriptures and meditation books. Place important writings and calligraphy on a small easel or elegant music stand.

OPPOSITE

Feathers displayed with reverence on soft pink walls inspire contemplation of the spirit. Each item in the home sanctuary has special meaning for the family.

HEALTHY RESTORATIONS

Living in an old house is like living with ancestors. You hear their voices in the creak of the floors and sense their presence in the chimney draft. Every detail tells a story: You draw strength and inspiration from the texture of the plaster, the filigree on the doorknob, and the pattern of the leaded window glass. By caring for these rooms, you nurture your heritage and also discover your soul.

Beyond the spiritual rewards, restoring an old house instead of building new has practical advantages. Older homes are often sturdier and more carefully crafted than houses built after the mid-twentieth century. Constructed of solid wood, brick, stone, and stucco, a historic building is less likely to contain particleboard, plastics, and other fume-producing synthetic materials. Moreover, saving a house from demolition means conserving natural resources, reducing refuse in landfills, and preventing the environmental harm that inevitably results from new construction.

These rewards do not come without hard work and considerable risks. Built before the rise in environmental consciousness, many older homes are poorly insulated and inefficiently heated. They may contain lead-based paints, asbestos, and other materials we now know to be highly toxic. Paint strippers, adhesives, cleaners, and other products commonly used in restoration are also hazardous. Indeed, old-house renovation involves so much stress and disruption that the process itself can undermine physical and psychological health.

A healthy restoration is not necessarily an exact historic re-creation. Working in partnership with your ancestors, you will want to balance respect for the past with the needs of the present. While you should not strip away details that give the home its charm, you will want to remove toxic elements and improve energy efficiency. To some extent, you may also want to adapt the original floor plan. Designed for very different lifestyles, older homes often used room arrangements that can seem convoluted, cramped, or impractical by modern standards. You may need to shift walls and open doorways to create larger bedrooms and bathrooms, more spacious closets, and more open living, dining, and kitchen areas. Or you may choose to make only minor changes, adapting your living patterns to the shape of the existing rooms. Your decisions will be healthy so long as they honor the past and also foster the physical and emotional well-being of all who enter.

Conservation Tips

Old-house restoration and environmental conservation go hand-in-hand. Preserve the architectural integrity of your older home and minimize waste by restoring instead of replacing as much as possible.

- Polish and reuse knobs and hinges.

- Rewire older light fixtures.

- Clean and reinstall historic switch plates, grilles, and radiators.

- Reglaze porcelain bathtubs and sinks.

- Refinish or paint old cabinets, doors, and moldings.

- Avoid wallboard; patch damaged plaster.

- Turn architectural salvage into furnishings.

OPPOSITE

To draw attention to historic details, furnish simply with crisp, clean lines and muted colors. Cotton slipcovers can be changed at a moment's notice for a whole new look.

"One sturdy house is worth
a hundred in ruins."

Kurdish proverb

Energy Efficiency

With high ceilings, single-pane windows, and scant insulation, an older home can gobble natural resources. Moreover, an outdated heating system is likely to be highly inefficient, wasting fuel, spewing pollution into the air, and failing to provide adequate warmth. Do not assume, however, that a house is inefficient simply because it is old. Before the invention of gas-fired boilers and air conditioning, our ancestors developed ingenious systems for heating and cooling. Your first step in reducing power consumption is to rediscover ways the original owners capitalized on the natural patterns of the sun and the seasons. Then, incorporate modern systems that do not undermine the architectural integrity of the building.

NATURAL HEATING AND COOLING

Trees and shrubbery do more than beautify; they insulate against heat and cold. Use plantings to filter sunlight in overheated rooms, and also to block chilling winter winds. High mounds of earth will also help insulate foundations. For soothing summertime shade, restore awnings and take family activities outside to the covered porch. For protection against both heat and cold, restore shutters or hang insulated draperies. Be sure that all windows open so you can capitalize on cross ventilation. Arrange rooms and schedule activities to correspond with nature's rhythms.

STOP DRAFTS

Weather stripping and caulking around doorjambs and windows will dramatically reduce heat loss. Also remember to patch damaged mortar on masonry buildings, fill cracks in wood siding, and seal gaps around exhaust fans, ventilators, and recessed light fixtures. Make sure your chimney has an airtight damper.

ADD INSULATION

Heat rises, and an attic or gable area that is not insulated will let warm air escape through the roof. As you add insulation, make sure to allow proper ventilation for the escape of condensation, which can cause moisture problems in the house. Exposed hot water pipes may also be wrapped with nontoxic insulation.

"If there is harmony in the home, there will be order in the nation."

Chinese proverb

INSTALL FANS

A whole-house exhaust system or ceiling fans can provide summer cooling and a distribution of heat during the winter. Fans require much less power than furnaces, boilers, and air conditioners.

SHIELD THE WINDOWS

Storm windows and modern replacement windows with double and triple panes will cut power usage by at least 50 percent. If modern windows will undermine the architectural integrity of the building, consider using less intrusive interior storm windows or protective film shields. For added protection, use insulating shades or curtains lined with heavy cotton felt.

FURNISH FOR THE SEASON

When the weather changes, change the slipcovers. Light-colored cotton is best when temperatures are hot. As the days cool, choose darker fabrics and move furniture closer together. To add insulation, move bookcases and other large furnishings against exterior walls. Plush wool area rugs will also help warm a chilly room. Make sure that rugs and furnishings do not block heat ducts.

ADD HUMIDIFIERS OR DEHUMIDIFIERS

Dry air feels cooler; moist air feels warmer. In a home that feels uncomfortably dry during the heating season, use a portable humidifier to add moisture to the air. In hot, humid weather, use a dehumidifier to reduce moisture.

UPGRADE THE HEATING SYSTEM

Modern furnaces and boilers are much more efficient than those used a decade or more ago. When you install a new system, make sure it is properly sized: A heater that is too large will turn on and off too often and use more fuel than a compact model. In addition, keeping the heating system clean and changing the filter often will improve energy efficiency. Rooms will also feel warmer if you put reflective foil behind the radiators and install wide windowsills to direct the heat.

ABOVE

Architects Scott Swanson and Dan Scully maintained the historic ambiance when they turned cramped nineteenth-century servants' quarters into a free-flowing great room for casual twenty-first century lifestyles.

Old-house Hazards

Old-house renovation is messy. Removing walls and pulling up floors is likely to stir up a toxic combination of dust, fumes, and other contaminants. Some of the materials used to remodel are also pollutants. Paints, wood strippers, finishes, adhesives, waxes, and cleaners contain petroleum distillates, formaldehyde, and other harmful chemicals. Before you begin work, make sure that you know the hazards and take steps to minimize the risks.

MOLD

A house that has been in disrepair is especially prone to infestations of molds, which can aggravate asthma and cause eye irritations, fever, headaches, and other health problems. Suspect a mold infestation if you see signs of fungal growths, smell musty odors, or discover evidence of water damage. Some standard building materials such as cellulose-based wallboard have nutrients that encourage mold growth. There is no practical way to completely eliminate mold. The solution is to reduce moisture inside the home and, as much as possible, remove materials that have been infected.

ASBESTOS

Asbestos is a strong, thin mineral fiber that was used for insulation and other building materials in many older homes. As long as it is not disturbed, asbestos need not be a concern. However, once the fibers become airborne, there is a risk that they will be inhaled. Prolonged exposure leads to cancer and lung diseases. In homes built before the 1980s, asbestos may be found in steam pipe insulation, resilient floor tiles, acoustical ceiling tiles, and cement roofing and siding shingles. Any material containing asbestos that is frayed or damaged should be either encapsulated in a special sealant or entirely removed by a trained professional.

Coping with Mold

- Check plumbing for leaks, and make prompt repairs.

- Keep rooms well ventilated.

- Use dehumidifiers and exhaust fans in moist areas.

- Keep shrubs and grass trimmed from around the foundation of the house.

- Move furniture away from walls and open closet doors to help air circulation.

- Wear a HEPA filter mask when cleaning moldy areas.

- Remove and replace flooded carpets, ceiling tiles, wallboard, and fabrics.

- Wash moldy woodwork with a weak bleach solution.

- Hire a professional to clean larger areas.

Coping with Asbestos

- As much as possible, stay out of rooms containing debris with asbestos.

- Avoid handling asbestos insulation.

- Do not sand, saw, drill, or scrape materials that contain asbestos.

- Do not use abrasive pads or brushes on asbestos flooring.

- Use a wet mop; do not sweep or vacuum debris that may contain asbestos.

- Hire an asbestos professional to do testing and removal.

"He who builds according to every man's advice will have a crooked house." **Danish proverb**

ABOVE

High, multipane windows are the crowning glory of this colonial room. Liberated from heavy drapery, they cast sunlight across pine plank flooring coated with a satin water-based finish.

CARBON MONOXIDE (CO)

Odorless, tasteless, and colorless, this silent killer is emitted by kerosene and oil heaters, gas stoves, wood stoves, and cigarettes. An older, poorly maintained furnace or boiler is especially prone to problems that could cause carbon monoxide poisoning. The first sign that this gas is present may be symptoms that mimic influenza: fatigue, headache, dizziness, nausea, mental confusion, and rapid pulse. Extended exposure will cause death. If CO poisoning is suspected, ventilate the area and get immediate medical help.

RADON

Radon is a colorless, odorless gas produced by the decay of uranium in rocks and soil. It is present to some degree everywhere, and any house, regardless of age, can have a radon problem. Small amounts are not dangerous, but years of exposure to excessive levels can cause lung cancer. The only way to determine whether your home has a problem is to measure the radon level. Consult with an environmental testing service or purchase a test kit from a home improvement store. Radon levels change from day to day and season to season. For the most accurate reading, choose a test that will remain in the home for at least ninety days.

"A single beam cannot support a great house."

Chinese proverb

Avoid Carbon Monoxide

- Keep chimneys clean.

- Have furnaces, water heaters, gas stoves, gas dryers, and other fuel-burning appliances inspected.

- Make sure that appliances are properly vented.

- Do not sleep in areas with gas or kerosene space heaters.

- Never run automobiles or other gasoline-powered engines inside a garage or other enclosed space.

- Do not use a gas stove for heating.

- Install a carbon monoxide alarm on each level of the home.

Reducing Radon

The design of your home will determine the best approach for reducing radon levels. Most systems use several techniques.

- Suction. Before it can enter the home, gas is piped from beneath the floor and vented outside.

- Sealing. Cracks in the foundation are sealed to block the flow of gas into the home, and also to prevent the loss of purified air.

- Pressurization. A powerful fan on an upper level creates enough pressure in the basement to prevent radon from entering the house.

- Natural Ventilation. Doors and windows are cracked open to circulate fresh air in the basement or crawl space. The contractor may install additional vents.

- Heat Recovery Ventilation. A heat exchanger is installed to increase ventilation and also to warm or cool the air.

ABOVE

Instead of replacing old fixtures, restore them with a fresh enamel finish. Pale colors help expand a smaller bathroom.

Coping with Lead Paint

- Use a testing kit from your home supply store to determine if your paint is lead-based.

- Remove doors, moldings, or other items that can be easily detached. Replace them with new materials or have them stripped at another location.

- Cover walls with plaster, paneling, or gypsum wallboard.

- Coat surfaces with a water-based lead paint sealant.

- Do not sand or saw materials coated with lead-based paint.

LEAD

In any older home, lead contamination is a serious concern. The toxic mineral enters the water from city service lines, lead piping in the home, and leaded solder used on pipes. Prior to the 1980s, lead was also used in many paints and finishes. When the paint flakes, peels, or is disrupted during home renovations, lead dust becomes airborne. Windowsills are prone to accumulations of lead dust because raising and lowering the windows wears at the paint. Young children are especially vulnerable to lead-related health problems.

To cleanse water of lead contaminants, install a whole-house filtration system. Removing lead-based paint from the home will be more difficult. If the painted surface shows no sign of damage, your best bet may be to simply apply a fresh coat of nontoxic paint. Repainting is not a permanent solution, however. In areas where there is wear, the original coat of lead paint will eventually loosen and cause more dust. For complete eradication, hire professionals who are trained to handle lead paint contamination.

Forunately, lead is no longer used in the manufacture of paint. However, the paints, varnishes, urethanes, strippers, and solvents you use during renovation may emit harmful fumes. In addition to ozone-depleting volatile organic compounds (VOCs), many modern paints and finishes contain chemicals to extend their shelf lives and, in some cases, fungicides and mildewcides that have strong odors.

To minimize fumes during a home renovation, read labels. Look for water-based products that are identified as low-VOC or zero-VOC and oil-based paints that are made from natural ingredients.

"By wisdom a house is built, and by understanding it is established; by knowledge the rooms are filled with all precious and pleasant riches."

The Bible (King James version), Prov. 24:3–4

Tips for Healthy Painting

- Choose low-VOC water-based paints and urethanes, or oil-based paints that are made from natural ingredients.

- Make sure that paints and finishes are not formulated with formaldehyde, halogenated solvents, aromatic hydrocarbons, mercury, or mercury compounds.

- Make sure that added pigments do not contain lead, cadmium, chromium, and their oxides.

- Never use spray paints.

- Keep fresh air circulating.

- Place a small bowl of vinegar in the room to reduce paint odors.

- Close doors or hang tarps to isolate the area from the rest of the house.

- Avoid chemical solvents such as mineral spirits; when they are essential, save and reuse them as much as possible.

- Minimize cleaning brushes and rollers; wrap them in plastic bags and reuse them the next day.

- Complete all painting before installing carpeting, ceiling tile, or other absorbent materials.

- Wait at least 48 hours before occupying a newly painted room.

- Give leftovers to a community organization.

- Check with your local waste management department to find out how to responsibly dispose of dirty cans and rags.

"The world is our house. Keep it clean." **Chinese proverb**

Healthy Paints and Finishes

LOW-VOC

Paints, stains, and varnishes labeled as low-VOC are water-based. Because they do not contain petroleum solvents, they create fewer fumes. Low-VOC paints also contain little or no formaldehyde or lead. Low-VOC paints do still have an odor while wet. Companies that manufacture low-VOC paints include Benjamin Moore, AFM Safecoat, ICI-Glidden, Cloverdale EcoLogic, and Carver Tripp Safe & Simple.

ZERO-VOC

Any paint with VOCs in the range of .5 grams per liter or less is labeled zero-VOC. However, some zero-VOC paints use colorants, biocides, and fungicides that slightly raise the level of fumes produced. Zero-VOC paints are available from AFM Safecoat, Earth Tech, ICI Lifemaster, ICI Decra-Shield, Enviro-Cote, Devoe Wonder Pure, Sherwin Williams, and Frazee Paint EnviroKote.

NATURAL PAINTS AND FINISHES

Made from plant oils and dyes, clay and chalk, milk casein, beeswax, and other natural ingredients, these oil-based paints have a pleasant fragrance and rarely pose problems for allergy sufferers. For natural paints, shop for these brand names: Livos and Livos Australia, Auro, EcoDesign, Tried & True, Weather-Bos, Old Fashioned Milk Paint Company, and Sawyer Finn Natural Milk Paint.

NONTOXIC PAINT STRIPPERS

Solutions strong enough to melt paint are likely to contain methylene chlorine, which can cause cancer. Paint strippers that are water-soluble take longer to work, but they are nontoxic and less harmful to the environment. Companies that manufacture nontoxic stripping agents include Specialty Environmental Technologies, W.M. Barr & Co., and Dumond Chemicals in New York.

Renovation Checklist

- Seal off the room. Post a warning sign and do not let children, pets, or other nonworkers into the area.

- Use plastic coverings on the floors. Remove shoes upon leaving the work area.

- Turn off heating and cooling systems. Avoid any ventilation that will disturb dust, fumes, and fibers into the rest of the house.

- Wear a HEPA-filter respirator while working.

- Do not eat or drink in the work area.

- Wash mops and rags thoroughly after each use.

- Read labels and follow instructions for safe, responsible cleanup and disposal.

Relax and Reflect...

Any major remodeling project will involve dust, debris, fumes, noise, and disruption. To maintain emotional equilibrium during this chaotic time, be sure to set aside a quiet, work-free zone where the family can continue normal activities. To prevent dust from spreading into the rest of the house, hang tarps over the doorways to work areas. Set aside a special area for tools and supplies, and be sure that the construction workers know which parts of the house are off-limits.

Keeping peace in the household will be easier if you can communicate openly with the workers. Show them which bathroom to use, where to wash their brushes, and where to park their trucks. If possible, establish hours: You may want to specify that work cannot continue past dinnertime. To contain noise and minimize disruptions, consider setting rules about playing radios and using the household telephone.

The larger the project, the greater are the chances that you will encounter unforeseen problems and delays. Expenses may escalate and a freshly painted room may not look quite the way you hoped. If you are doing the work yourself, you are likely to feel exhausted and discouraged.

Before renovating the house undermines the health of everyone in it, be sure to take time out for relaxation and reflection. Enjoy some meals at your favorite restaurant. Spend a weekend at a romantic bed and breakfast inn. Talk about why you began the project and what its completion will mean for you, your family, and the community.

Also remember to give workers a break from routine. Turn work into a celebration as you step back to admire accomplishments and savor the excitement of the project. In the long run, it will be far more important to build your home on a foundation of camaraderie and enjoyment than to meet a deadline or paint a perfect wall.

"Home wasn't built in a day."

Jane Sherwood Ace (1905–1974), U.S. actress and comedian

RECOVERING BEAUTY AND JOY

Strong emotion creates energy that lingers long after the events have passed. A sense of foreboding or an aura of profound sadness may pervade the rooms. Or when the energy is joyful, you may feel a rush of serenity. Bubbling up from your past—or from the past of a previous occupant—these sensations will affect your physical health and emotional well-being as much as the air you breathe.

A house is happy when its occupants have lived there with peace and joy. Unhappy energies, however, come from many sources. Grief or unfulfilled yearnings will cast emotional shadows in the sunniest rooms. A traumatic death or illness will trigger a ripple effect that can last for centuries. Years after the rubble has been cleared away, storms, fires, earthquakes, and other catastrophic events continue to bring despair.

In the aftermath of the devastating terrorist attack in New York City, the world-renowned designer Clodagh made her city penthouse an experimental workshop where she explored methods for physical and spiritual cleansing. An environmental consultant tested the air and water, a *feng shui* practitioner balanced the energies, and spiritual leaders performed space-cleansing rituals. Through the prolonged process, Clodagh found that re-creating the home is actually a way of re-creating the life. Each stage requires extended periods of reflection and self-examination, a time when you are actually "dusting between the ears."

While you need not practice all the procedures taken by Clodagh, removing harmful energies from a troubled home will always begin with purging the past. Take time for quiet contemplation and decide what is truly important in your life. Use this opportunity to clear away belongings that sap at your spirit, evoke unhappy memories, or have simply outgrown their usefulness. Get rid of clothes that no longer fit your self-image or that carry unpleasant associations. Recycle outdated magazines and catalogs, and give away books you are unlikely to read. File or throw away old bills and other paperwork. Dispose of chipped china and glassware, and repair or throw away anything that is torn or broken. Take a careful inventory of furnishings and collectibles, and remove any item that stirs sadness, anger, or remorse. By freeing yourself of these possessions, you make way for new joy in your life.

"There is no such thing as an inanimate object."

Clodagh, contemporary designer

OPPOSITE

Carefully selected details at the threshold take on symbolic meaning. Here, handcrafted rakes on the wall "clear away" the past and ward off evil, while fresh sunflowers suggest vitality and stabilize earth energy.

Purify the Space...

SWEEP AWAY GRIEF

After the space has been cleared, it is time to launch a thorough cleansing. In some cultures, ritual sweeping is embodied with mystical powers to drive away evil. Starting at the entrance, move clockwise around the room, rhythmically sweeping dust and cobwebs from floors, shelves, moldings, and ceilings. Next, move clockwise again, mopping the floors with hot water scented with crumpled sage leaf and pine or eucalyptus oil. This type of ritual activity does more than remove dirt; the rhythmic motion is psychologically satisfying and also helps sweep away negativity.

ADD FRESH WATER

Water is a powerful symbol of life and purity. To prevent life energy from draining away, promptly repair leaking pipes and dripping faucets. Change the water in flower vases every day and make sure that aquariums are fresh. Consider adding an indoor fountain; even a small tabletop fountain will bring pleasant sounds and soothing associations.

INVITE NATURE INDOORS

Living plants represent rebirth. If plants in the room are straggly, move them outdoors to recover or to compost. Bring in new, vital plants in a variety of shapes and sizes. Put forsythia branches in jugs of water to invite fresh blooms, or fill baskets with aromatic pinecones. A basket of shells or a small arrangement of timeworn stones will help ease the pain of troubling memories.

Psychic Healing

To heal a home after the end of a treasured relationship:

- Purchase a new bed.

- Move photographs of your former lover out of the bedroom.

- Rearrange the furniture.

- Choose a new color scheme.

- Replace or reupholster furnishings you shared together.

- Get rid of gifts and mementos, or store them out of sight.

- Give away clothing or jewelry that remind you of the relationship.

- Fill rooms with living plants and other symbols of life and renewal.

- Hold a ceremony to bury the past and celebrate your new life.

HEAL WITH COLOR

Scientists have long known that color affects mood and triggers specific physiological responses. Each hue emits a unique wavelength frequency that travels neurological pathways to our pineal glands and stimulates a definable response. With this in mind, you may want to select colors not only for their aesthetic beauty but also for their healing properties. Seek a new color scheme that lifts your spirits, or select deeper shades of the existing colors. If you don't want to change the walls, consider painting the trim and a few key furnishings in a contrasting shade. To avoid fumes, choose a water-based, low-VOC paint or a paint made from natural ingredients.

> "Red is the ultimate cure for sadness."

Bill Blass, U.S. fashion designer

Healing Colors

Every color has resonance. In a landmark study on color psychology, the noted researcher Faber Birren found that specific hues have clearly defined therapeutic benefits. Other scientists have added to Faber's ideas, reporting successes in using color to treat numerous ailments. Some theorists also say that the colors we prefer suggest our subconscious search for the vibrations we need to heal ourselves.

Red

Red is the most passionate of colors. It stimulates brainwave activity and increases heart rate, respiration, and blood pressure. Most people will find red over-stimulating if it is used in excess. However, modified tones such as maroon, rose, and pink are warm and deeply emotional. A wisp of rosy hues will relax tired muscles and relieve tension. Pink is also an appetite suppressant and is sometimes used in diet therapy.

Orange

Orange is not as intense as red, but has many of the same properties. It casts a cheerful glow and helps relieve fatigue. Orange also stimulates the appetite and the digestive system, and is very appropriate for dining areas. Pure orange may seem too vibrant to use in quantity, but orange-tinged colors such as peach, salmon, apricot, coral, melon, and some earth tones are mellow and inviting.

Yellow

Yellow is appealing for its ability to make dark spaces seem brighter. Rooms painted with yellow hues will lift the spirits and relieve fatigue. Some scientists also claim that yellow is helpful for treating bowel and intestinal problems.

Green

Combining the warmth of yellow with the peacefulness of blue, green connotes life energy. Soothing and neutral, it eases stress and relieves muscle tension. Green is ideal for rooms to be used for concentration, meditation, and relaxation. Researchers have found green tones helpful for people suffering from depression, anxiety, and nervousness.

Blue

Soothing and nurturing, blue is the polar opposite of red. It lowers the blood pressure, decreases respiration, and soothes inflammations. Pale blues evoke the sky and suggest peace and harmony. Darker shades are subduing and encourage contemplation. Blue tones can also connote sadness and may become a slight depressant.

Purple

Combining the passion of red with the tranquility of blue, purple neither stimulates nor relaxes. It is a mysterious color that some people may find unsettling. Nevertheless, researchers claim that purple tones may be helpful for treating migraines and nervous disorders. As the hues deepen, they enhance calm contemplation.

Black

Darkness need not mean despair. Although Western cultures associate black with death and mourning, the color can also suggest power, strength, and sophistication. Use ebony hues with white or a single bold color to strengthen your spirit and boost self-confidence.

White

Like the light at the end of life's tunnel, white may be associated with death or with spirituality. In some cultures, white is the color of mourning; in others, it represents cleanliness, purity, and simplicity. Rooms painted white will capture colors from lampshades, curtains, and bedcovers. Subtle shifts in tone and texture will add interest to an all-white room

ABOVE

Combining all colors of the spectrum, white cleanses and purifies. A well-placed mirror draws pleasing views into the home. To soften sharp corners, choose plants that have large, rounded leaves.

OPPOSITE

An uncluttered life begins with a commitment to live simply. Deep green accents suggest growth and fertility.

Bless Your House

A traditional house blessing ritual may include any combination of these elements:

Water

Mix rue, vervain, and valerian, or other healing herbs with seawater. Sprinkle the herbal water in rooms and around the foundation of the house.

Sea Salt

Many traditions believe salt will create a protective shield that evil spirits cannot penetrate. Sprinkle sea salt inside the house and also around the foundation.

Smoke

In Native American traditions, sagebrush, cedar, sweetgrass, and tobacco are burned in a small pot or open shell. The herbs may also be bundled with cotton, forming a "smudge stick." Slowly walk counterclockwise around the edge of each room, fanning the herbal smoke. The smoke will wash away energies left behind by former occupants.

Fire

Flame represents cleansing. To purify the space and also to honor and celebrate the home, hold the ceremony by candlelight. For natural scents, choose candles made with herbs or essential oils.

Sounds

Nearly every culture uses some type of rhythmic, repetitive sound to drive away evil spirits and bring happy vibrations. Ring bells, play drums or chimes, or clap loudly in unison.

Starting Over...

Our homes are manifestations of our spirits. The dwellings we choose and the way we decorate them reflect who we are and what we hope to become. In turn, our personalities are profoundly influenced by our surroundings. In a sense, our homes are our destinies.

The psychologist Carl Jung viewed the home as a symbol for the self. In his autobiographical *Memories, Dreams, Reflections,* he described the gradual construction of his castle-like home on Lake Zurich, and likened the evolution of its towers and annexes to the development of his psyche. Drawing on Jung's concepts, Clare Cooper Marcus, a professor of architecture at the University of California in Berkeley, observed that furnishings, wall color, and other aspects of interior design reveal inner conflicts and also point the way to their resolution.

Removing negative energies from a troubled home may be as simple as rearranging the furniture. Try placing chairs and sofas at diagonals, and move some items into different rooms. Consider the ancient principles of *feng shui* or *vástu shástra,* but also listen closely to your own instincts. You may find that you can rest more comfortably after moving the bed away from the door, and that you work more productively after shifting the position of your desk. Almost magically, adding a new piece of furniture can manifest new realities: To open your life to a relationship, place an extra chair at the dining table.

Altering the physical appearance of a room will also help change its emotional tenor. To change the look of furnishings, add slipcovers and cotton throws. Use toss pillows and area rugs to introduce new colors. Also change the picture frames and lampshades, or paint the old ones. Install new window shades, or use paint, stencils, or fabric ribbons to transform existing shades.

Within the confines of the walls and ceilings, your home is yours to recreate. Consider changing doorknobs, cabinet pulls, and other hardware. Install new light fixtures, or change the bulbs to a different color or wattage. Treat the kitchen and bathroom to new faucets, and replace old countertops with earth-hewn stone.

ABOVE

*Healing energies flow freely through rooms
without carpeting or heavy draperies. Red
orchids, green glass, and fresh fruit symbolize
rebirth.*

Even the most fundamental architectural details are open to reinterpreta-
tion. For a dramatic new beginning, change the baseboards and door and window trim. Install cove moldings along the ceiling, replace the doors, and build
shelves, cabinets, or window seats. Rescued from demolished buildings,
columns, corbels, brackets, and other architectural salvage will bring in the
energies of the original craftsmen and can restore the happier moments of a
bygone era.

Whether you are changing a few small details or rebuilding your house
from inside out, make sure that you listen to your inner voice. Take your time
and experiment with new colors and arrangements, and choose a design plan
that feels completely comfortable. Avoid meaningless, unnecessary decoration, but do surround yourself with details that lift your spirits. Everywhere
you look, you should see something that brings you peace.

Healing Ceremonies

Over the centuries, the peoples of many nations have developed a rich array of ceremonies to clear the air of harmful energies and invite good fortune. In ancient China, *feng shui* practitioners performed *chi* adjustment rituals. Native Americans burned potent herbs and chanted invocations. Believers in the Wiccan tradition used spells and fragrant potions, while early Christians relied on holy water, incense, and bells.

Many of the old practices continue today, bringing comfort to families who want to close the door on the past and celebrate new beginnings. A formal house blessing is like a wedding in that it publicly affirms a commitment to begin a new life in accordance to treasured values. A formal blessing may also resemble a funeral in that it can bring closure and assist in the healing process.

If you choose to hold a blessing ceremony, you may borrow from ancient traditions or create a ritual that reflects your spiritual beliefs. A priest, rabbi, shaman, *feng shui* practitioner, or other spiritual leader can assist in preparing and conducting the event. Choose words and symbols that are especially meaningful to you and your family. Regardless of the details, the ceremony will be healing so long as it is conducted with thoughtfulness and respect.

"…we all, to some degree, display in the physical environment messages from the unconscious about who we are, who we were, and who we might become."

Claire Cooper Marcus, *House as a Mirror of Self*

OPPOSITE

Any room can be transformed by adding abundant foliage, a treasured sculpture, and fresh upholstery in a bright new pattern. A well-placed mirror will capture pleasing views and brighten dark corners.

Prayers, Incantations, and Songs

Every house blessing draws its power from the commitment of the people who live there. To assure that the ritual has lasting effect, it is important to speak, sing, or chant your hopes, dreams, and intentions. Choose words written by your spiritual leader, select passages from a holy book, or write your own. Verbalize warm, loving wishes for the house and also for everything and everyone in the house. Address your desire to live in harmony with nature and to provide shelter that nurtures and heals. Cast these words in the form of a song or a mantra, or simply recite them with loud conviction. To seal your commitment, invite relatives, friends, and neighbors to join you in song and prayer.

As a highlight of the ceremony, you may want to celebrate and honor your re-created home by giving it a name. Find a word that symbolizes harmony and beauty. Or, show love for your home by giving it your family name. Place the name at the entrance along with a symbol of protection. In this way, the house will bring comfort, joy, and healing to all who come inside.

OPPOSITE

Tall fresh tulips and glowing candles celebrate
new beginnings.

Blessing from Baha'u'llah, Founder of the Baha'i Faith

Blessed is the spot, and the house, and the place, and the city, and the heart, and the mountain, and the refuge, and the cave, and the valley, and the land, and the sea, and the island, and the meadow where mention of God hath been made, and His praise glorified.

Navajo Blessing

May my house be in harmony; from my head, may it be happy; to my feet, may it be happy; Where I lie, may it be happy; all above me, may it be happy; all around me, may it be happy.

Irish Blessing

God bless the corners of this house
And be the lintel blest
And bless the hearth and bless
   the board
And bless each place of rest
And bless each door that opens wide
To stranger as to kin
And bless each crystal window pane
That lets the starlight in
And bless the rooftop overhead
And every sturdy wall.
The peace of man, the peace of God
The peace of love on all.

BUYER'S GUIDE: RESOURCES FOR CREATING A HEALTHY HOME

The suppliers listed here are just a sampling of the numerous companies that offer resources for creating healthy, eco-friendly homes. Many have world-wide distribution centers or international mail order via the Internet.

APPLIANCES

ASKO
Web site: www.asko.dk
Energy-efficient dishwashers, washers, and dryers

Bosch
Tel: (49) (0) 180-530-4050 (Netherlands);
 (800) 944-3904 (USA)
Fax: (49) (0) 180-133-5308 (Netherlands)
Web site: www.bosch-hausgeraete.de
Condenser washer dryer and energy-efficient dishwashers

Danby
Tel: (519) 837-0920 (Canada);
 (419) 425-8627 (USA)
Fax: (519) 837-0449 (Canada);
 (419) 425-8629 (USA)
Web site: www.danby.com
Compact refrigerators and other energy-efficient appliances

Equator Corporation
Equator Plaza
10067 Timber Oak Drive
Houston, TX 77080, USA
Tel: (713) 464-3422
Fax: (713) 464-2151
Web site: www.equatorappl.com
Distributes the European "clothes processor" combination washer and dryer and other compact, water and energy saving appliances

Fisher & Paykel
78 Springs Road
East Tamaki, Auckland, New Zealand
Tel: (64) (9) 273-0600
Fax: (64) (9) 273-0538
Web site: www.fp.co.nz
The DishDrawer dishwasher and other eco-friendly appliances

Foron
EFS Hausgeräte GmbH
Salzstraße 1, D-09113 Chemnitz, Germany
Tel: (49) 03-7133-87100
Fax: (49) 03-7133-87140
Eco-friendly washer recycles rinse water

Sun Frost
PO Box 1101
Arcata, CA 95518, USA
Tel: (707) 822-9095
Fax: (707) 822-6213
E-mail: info@sunfrost.com
Web site: www.sunfrost.com
Energy-efficient refrigerators

The Staber System 2000
4800 Homer Ohio Lane
Groveport, OH 43125, USA
Tel: (800) 848-6200; (614) 836-5995
Email: info@staber.com
"Energy-efficient Top-Load Horizontal Washing System"

Thermor
Web site: www.thermor.fr
Induction cooktops

BATHROOM

U.S. Standard
PO Box 6820
1 Centennial Plaza
Piscataway, NJ 08855, USA
Tel: (800) 223-0068
Web site: www.U.S.standard.com
The ergonomic "Slipper Tub" and other plumbing fixtures

Belhydro
Zwaaikomstraat 72
8800 Roeselare, Belgium
Tel: (32) (0)5124-0508
Fax: (32) (0)5124-6280
Web site: www.belhydro.be
Whirlpools, bathtubs, steam enclosures, saunas

BJ Industries
2900 Wind Cave Court
Burnsville, MN 55337, USA
Tel: (952) 890-3870
Fax: (952) 890-1156
Web site: www.bjindustries.com
Adjust-a-Sink System

Duravit
Werderstrasse 36
D-78132 Hornberg, Germany
Tel: (49) 78-3370-0
Fax: (49) 78-3370-289
Web site: www.duravit.com
Bathroom sinks, toilets, and accessories

Ideal Building Material Co., Ltd.
184, Xiangang Road, Songgang Town
Nanhai, Guangdong, China
Tel: (86) 757-5503121
Fax: (86) 757-5500121
Web site: www.china-ideal.com
Modular glass shower enclosures

Kohler
444 Highland Drive
Kohler, WI 53044, USA
Tel: (800) 456-4537
Web site: www.kohler.com
Deep soaking tubs and other luxury fixtures

Laufen International, Switzerland
Web site: www.laufen.com
Ceramic tiles and bathroom fixtures

Marc Sanitation Pvt. Ltd.
A - 2, S.M.A. Co-op Industrial Estate
G.T. Karnal Road
Delhi, 110 033, India
Tel: (91) (11) 743-3490-91
Fax: (91) (11) 721-9295
Web site: www.marcindia.com
Faucets, mixers, single lever fixtures

Pombo: Indúústria Metalúúrgica, Lda.
Av. da Junqueira, 330, Francelos
4406-901 Valadares, Portugal
Tel: (351) 22-753-9024
Fax: (351) 22-753-2883
Web site: www.pombo.pt
Luxury brass rails and other bathroom accessories

Porcher France
Paris Nord II, 161 rue de la Belle Etoile
95920 Roissy Charles de Gaulle Cedex, France
Tel: (33) (1) 493-828-00
Fax: (33) (1) 493-828-28
Web site: www.porcher.com
Baths, sinks, and fixtures

Sanijet Corporate Offices
1461 S. Beltline Road, Suite 100
Coppell, TX 75019, USA
Tel: (972) 745-2283
Fax: (972) 745-2285
Web site: www.sanijet.com
Manufactures pipeless whirlpool tubs

Showerlux U.K. Limited
Sibree Road
Coventry, West Midlands UK CV3 4FD, UK
Tel: (44) (024) 76-639400
Fax: (44) (024) 76-305457
Web site: www.duscholux.com
Product line includes the Bodyzone combined steam and shower room

The Steam & Sauna Connection
1500 SW 2nd Place
Pompano Beach, FL 33069, USA
Tel: (954) 784-7279
Fax: (954) 941-0152
Web site: www.steamsaun.com

Toto KikiUsa/Toto Ltd.
1-1 Nakashima 2-chome, Kokurakita-ku
Kitakyushu, Fukuoka 802-8601, Japan
Tel: (81) 93-951-2707;
      (770) 282-8686 (USA)
Fax: (81) 93-922-6789;
      (770) 282-8697 (USA)
Web site: www.totousa.com
Toilet/bidet units with wash and dry functions and other automatic controls

Whitewater Specialties Ltd., Canada
Tel: (44) 1274-603970 (UK);
      (800) 882-7638 (USA)
Fax: (44) 1274 603967 (UK)
Web site: www.softbathtubs.com
Manufactures "Soft Tubs" padded bathtubs

CABINETS AND STORAGE

California Closets
1000 Fourth Street, Suite 800
San Rafael, CA 94901
Tel: (800) 274-6754
Web site: www.californiaclosets.com

Hettich International/Hettich Amercia, L.P.
6225 Shiloh Road
Alpharetta, GA 30005, USA
Tel: (770) 887-3733
Web site: www.hettich.com
Fittings, hardware, and drawer systems; creator of the Kitchen Concept 2010 project for ergonomic design

Neff Kitchen Manufacturers, Ltd.
6 Melanie Drive
Brampton, ON L6T 4K9, Canada
Tel: (905) 791-7770; (800) 268-4527
Web site: www.neffweb.com
Wood and metal cabinets made of nontoxic materials

CLEANING PRODUCTS

AquaSapone
6 Durham Street
Mayfield NSW 2304, Australia
Tel: (61) 02-4960-1462
Fax: (1) 781-998-8427
Web site: www.soap.it
Environmentally friendly, natural soaps, shampoos, and household products

Bio-Kleen Products
508 Harrison Street
Kalamazoo, MI 49007, USA
Tel: (800) 240-5536
Web site: www.biokleen.com/contact.cfm
Environmentally safe cleaning products

Chemical Sensitivity Living
377 Wilbur Avenue, Suite 213
Swansea, MA 02777, USA
Tel: (508) 678-7293
Fax: (718) 889-2608
Web site: www.chemsenlvng.com
Cleaning products and cotton bedding for persons with multiple chemical sensitivities

Coconut Coast Natural Products
PO Box 1173
5651 Kawaihau Road
Kapaa, Kauai, HI 96746, USA
Tel: (808) 822-2772
Fax: (808) 822-0350
Web site: www.ccnphawaii.com
Manufactures natural bathing soap which has no synthetic compounds

GreenMarketPlace
5801 Beacon Street, Suite #2
Pittsburgh, PA 15217, USA
Tel: (800) 59-EARTH
Web site: www.greenmarketplace.com
All-natural cleaning products

Janices
Tel: (800) 526-4237
Fax: (973) 691-05459
Web site: www.janices.com
Unscented, natural laundry, dishwashing, and cleaning products

Kokopelli's Green Market
PO Box 1899
Broomfield, CO 80038, USA
Tel: (800) 210-0202
Fax: (303) 404-2008
Chemically free trash bags, pet products, and other household goods

The Natural Soap Company
2d Maryland
Wells-next-the-Sea
Norfolk NR23 1LY, UK
Tel: (44) 01328-711717
Fax: (44) 01328-713003
Web site: www.naturalsoap.co.uk
Manufactures herbal bathing soap which has no synthetic compounds

Orange Glo
PO Box 70171
Eugene, OR 97401, USA
Tel: (800) 672-6456
Fax: (541) 895-3295
Web site: http://www.GoGlo.com
All-natural, cruelty-free household products

Organics of OZ, Inc.
PO Box 3071
Costa Mesa, CA 92628, USA
Tel: (714) 241-1164
Fax: (714) 546-8844
Web site: www.organicsofoz.com/USA/TN/tnpage2.html
Organic cleaning products and household goods

Vermont Soapworks
616 Exchange Street
Middlebury, VT 05753, USA
Tel: (802) 388-4302
Fax: (802) 388-7471
Web site: www.vermontsoap.com
Nontoxic personal care

Chauncey's Architectural
15/16 Feeder Road, St. Philips
Bristol, UK
Tel: (44) 0117-971-3131
Web site: www.chauncey.co.uk
Recycled antique wood flooring

Classical Flagstones
Lower Ledge Farm
Dyrham
Wiltshire SN14 8EY, UK
Tel: (44) 0122-531-6759
Fax: (44) 0117-303-9088
Web site: www.classical-flagstones.com
Limestone and flagstone flooring

CV Dutanda Borneo Mandiri Export
jl. kakap 56-58
semarang jawa tengah 50173, Indonesia
Tel: (62) 24-356-9701
Fax: (62) 24-358-8144
Web site: www.woodflooring.cjb.net
*Recycled antique wood, cork, and custom
wood flooring*

Eco-Products
Building Division
3655 Frontier Avenue
Boulder, CO 80301, USA
Tel: (303) 449-1876
Fax: (303) 449-1877
Web site: www.ecoproducts.com
*Environmentally friendly floors, including porcelain
tiles, cork, and natural linoleum*

LASSCO Flooring
41 Maltby Street
London SE1 3PA, UK
Tel: (44) 0207-237-4488
Fax: (44) 0207-237-2564
Web site: www.lassco.co.uk/floor
Custom wood, bamboo, and salvaged flooring

Anna French Ltd.
343 Kings Road
London SW3 5GS, UK
Tel: (44) 0207-351-1126
To the Trade Only

Brampton House Solid Wood Furniture
10086 Hurontario Street
Unit # 11, White Rose Plaza
Brampton, Ontario L7A 1E5, Canada
Web site: www.bramptonhousesolidwoodfurniture.com

Carolina Morning Designs
5790 Highway 80 South
Burnsville, NC 28714, USA
Tel: (888) 267-5366
Web site: www.zafu.net
*Designs and manufactures traditional meditation
furniture*

Harmony In Design
2050 South Dayton Street
Denver CO 80231, USA
Tel: (303) 337-7728
Fax: (303) 337-8247
Web site: www.harmonyindesign.com
Yoga, meditation, and ergonomic furniture

Heritage Wood Furniture, Inc.
R.D. #1, Box 449, Route 6
Mansfield, PA 16933, USA
Tel: (570) 662-7488
Web site: www.heritagewoodfurniture.com
Natural wood furnishings

IKEA
Web site: www.ikea.com
*Simple ergonomic furniture designs; world-wide
distribution*

Maine Cottage Furniture
Tel: (207) 846-1430
Fax: (207) 846-0602
Web site: www.mainecottage.com
Painted wood furnishings

R.O.O.M.
Alstromergaten 20, Box 49024
SE-100 28 Stockholm, Sweden
Tel: (46) 8-692-5000
Fax: (46) 8-692-5060
Web site: www.room.se
Furnishings, closet organizers, and cabinets

Sentient™
244 Fifth Avenue, Suite 2117
New York, NY 10010, USA
Tel/Fax: (212) 772-0112
Web site: www.meditationchair.com
Meditation chairs and other ergonomic furnishings

Solid Woods Inc.
40 West Jubal Early Drive
Winchester, VA 22601, USA
Tel: (540) 662-0647
Web site: www.swuf.com/index2.asp
Unfinished wood furniture

Spiegel
Tel: (800) 527-1577
Web site: www.spiegel.com
Lightweight, adaptable furnishings via mail order

Strictly Wood Furniture Company
301 South McDowell Street, Suite 811
Charlotte, NC 28204, USA
Tel: (800) 278-2019
Fax: (704) 331-8359
Web site: www.strictlywoodfurniture.com

U.S. Formulating & Manufacturing
Web site: www.afmsafecoat.com
*Safecoat paints for those who suffer from chemical
sensitivity*

Auro Organic Paints
Unit 2 Pamphillions Farm
Purton End, Debden, Saffron Walden
Essex CB11 3JT, UK
Tel: (44) 0179-9543 077
Fax: (44) 0179-9542 187
Web site: www.auro.com
*Solvent-free, water-based natural paints and primers,
finishes, stains, and adhesives*

Benjamin Moore & Co.
51 Chestnut Ridge Road
Montvale, NJ 07645, USA
Tel: (800) 344-0400
Web site: www.benjaminmoore.com
Low and No Biocide formulations are available

Carver Tripp Safe & Simple (Parks Corporation)
One West Street
Fall River, MA 02720
Tel: (800) 225-8543
Web site: www.parkscorp.com
*Low-VOC and low-toxin water-based stains and
clear finishes*

Chem-Safe Products
PO Box 33023
San Antonio, TX 78265, USA
Tel: (210) 657-5321
Nontoxic latex paint

Cloverdale EcoLogic
6950 King George Highway
Surrey, British Columbia V3W4Z1, Canada
Tel: (604) 596-6261
Fax: (604) 597-2677
Web site: www.cloverdalepaint.com
Low-VOC flat, eggshell, semi-gloss interior latex

Devoe Wonder Pure
ICI Paints North America
925 Euclid Avenue
Cleveland, OH 44115, USA
Web site: www.devoepaint.com
Zero-VOC paints

Dumond Chemicals, Inc.
1501 Broadway
New York, NY 10036, USA
Tel: (212) 869-6350
Web site: www.dumondchemicals.com
Water-soluble, noncaustic, nontoxic biodegradable paint strippers

Dutch Boy
Tel: (800) 828-5669
Web site: www.dutchboy.com
Low-odor paints and primers

Earth Tech
PO Box 1325
Arvada, CO 80001, USA
Tel: (303) 465-1537
Web site: www.earthtechinc.com
Zero-VOC paints, and nontoxic clear and pigmentable finishes

EcoDesign Co.
1365 Rufina Circle
Santa Fe, NM 87507, USA
Tel: (505) 438-3448
Fax: (505) 438-0199
Web site: www.bioshieldpaint.com
Natural paints and finishes

The Glidden Company
Tel: (800) 454-3336
Fax: (800) 834-6077
Web site: www.glidden.com
Latext and oil/alkyd paints. Glidden is owned by ICI Paints.

ICI Paints North America
925 Euclid Avenue
Cleveland, OH 44115, USA
Web site: www.icipaints.com
Low-VOC paints

Kelly Moore
Web site: www.kellymoore.com
"Enviro-Cote" nontoxic paints

Livos Phytochemistry of America, Inc.
PO Box 1740
Mashpee, MA 02649, USA
Tel: (508) 477-7955
Fax: (508) 477-7988
Web site: www.livos.com; www.lisp.com.au/~livos (Australia)
Organic paint, stains, oils, and waxes using all natural ingredients

The Old Fashioned Milk Paint Company
436 Main Street
P.O. Box 222
Groton, MA 01450, USA
Tel: (978) 448-6336
Fax: (978) 448-2754
Web site: www.milkpaint.com
Nontoxic paint made with milk protein, lime, clay, and earth pigments

Sawyer Finn Company
1600 Genessee
Kansas City, MO 64102, USA
Tel: (816) 421-3321
Web site: www.sawyerfinn.com
Nontoxic milk paint in powder form

Sherwin Williams
Tel: (800) 4-SHERWIN
Web site: www.sherwin-williams.com
"Healthspec" nontoxic paint

Weather-Bos
Tel: (800) 664-3978
Web site: www.weatherbos.com
Natural stains, finishes and paints

PURIFICATION: AIR

Absolute Air Cleaners & Purifiers
401 Meadow Road
Durango, CO 81301, USA
Tel: (970) 259-3998
Fax: (970) 259-3557
HEPA air filters

The Air Sponge Filter Company
3613 NW 124th Avenue
Coral Springs, FL 33065, USA
Tel: (800) 757-1836
Web site: www.dustless.com

PURIFICATION: WATER

Culligan International Co.
One Culligan Parkway
Northbrook, IL 60062, USA
Tel: (847) 205-6000
Web site: www.culligan.com
Reverse-osmosis filter systems

Filtrex Corporation
11 Hansen Avenue
New City, NY 10956
Tel: (914) 638-9708
Web site: www.filtrex.com
Filters for lead, scale, bacteria, and chlorine

Global Environmental Technologies, Inc
PO Box 8839
1001-1003 South 10th Street
Allentown, PA 18105, USA
Tel: (610) 821-4901
Fax: (610) 821-5507
Web site: www.terraflo.com
KDF filtration system

Kiss International
1475 12th Steet East
Palmetto, FL 34221, USA
Tel: (813) 722-3999
Web site: www.purewater4u.com/store/kiss.shtml
Reverse-osmosis filter systems

STONE PRODUCTS

FormWorks
111 Candy Apple Court
Cary, NC 27513, USA
Tel: (919) 434-5339
Fax: (253) 423-7369
Web site: www.homestead.com/formworks/index.html
Concrete countertops

Green Mountain Soapstone
780 East Hubbardton Rd.
Castleton, VT 05735, USA
Tel: (802) 468-5636
Fax: (802) 468-8968
Web site: www.greenmountainsoapstone.com

M. Teixeira Soapstone
465-B River Drive
Garfield, NJ 07026, USA
Tel: (973) 478-1001
Fax: (973) 478-1001
Web site: www.soapstones.com

Rock Revelations
1 Cransley Hill
Broughton
Kettering NN14 1NB, UK
Tel: (44) 0153-679-1737
Fax: (44) 0153-679-1536
Web site: http://www.rock-revelations.co.uk/
Granite and marble

Stoneworks of Italy
11810 Gray's Corner Road
PO Box 458
Berlin, MD 21811, USA
Tel: (410) 213-1291
Fax: (410) 213-1290
Web site: www.stoneworksofitaly.com
Enameled lava stone

Stone Selection, Inc.
3382 Enterprise Avenue
Hayward, CA 94545, USA
Tel: (510) 782-3000
Fax: (510) 782-1383
Marble, limestone, and lavastone

DiLana

Gallery/Workshop
50 Salisbury Street
PO Box 2927
Christchuch, New Zealand
Phone/Fax: (64) 3-366-5866
Web site: www.dilana.co.nz
All-natural wool carpeting

Earthsake

1425 4th Street
Berkeley, CA 94710, USA
Tel: (510) 848-5023
Web site: www.earthsake.com
Organic fabrics

Glen Eden Wool Carpet

430 Union Grove Road
Calhoun, GA 30701, USA
Tel: (800) 843-1728
Fax: (706) 629-4551
Web site: www.glen-eden.com
All-natural wool carpeting

Köppel AG

Fabrikstrasse 10
Hägendorf, Solothurn 4614, Switzerland
Tel: (41) 62-209-2006
Fax: (41) 62-209-2009
Organic cotton garments and fashions

Kyrenia Textile Ltd.

Industrial Estate
Kyrenia, Mersin 10 Turkey, Cyprus
Tel: (90) 392-822-2084
Fax: (90) 392-822-2091
Organic home textiles

Marimekko Oyi

Puusepankatu 4
Finland 00810 Helsinki, Finland
Tel: (358) 9-75871
Web site: www.marimekko.fi
To the trade only; clothing, interior decoration, and accessories

Lamb Rugs

4140 Locust Hill Road
Taylors, SC 29687, USA
Tel: (864) 895-4468
Web site: users.talstar.com/dray/lamb
All-natural wool carpeting

Peru Naturtex Partners

Sidro F-2 Vallecito
Vallecito, Arequipa, Peru
Tel: 51-54-24-7221
Fax: 51-54-22-7128
Web site: www.interplace.com.pe/pakucho.htm
Contract manufacturer and sourcing for eco-friendly home textiles

Siltex Mills Ltd.

10 Robinson Street
Winnipeg, R2W 4C6, Canada
Tel: (204) 582-2371
Fax: (204) 582-3071
Web site: www.siltex.com
Organic fabrics

Sushant Apparels Pvt. Ltd.

196/22 Aiswarya Commercial Complex
T.V. Swamy Road West, R.S. Puram
Coimbatore, Tamil Nadu 641002, India
Tel: (91) 422-542850
Web site: www.sushantcotton.com
Eco-friendly bed, bath, and table linens and other all-natural textiles

Texture

84 Stoke Newington Church Street
London, N16 0AP, UK
Tel: (44) 0207-241-0990
Fax: (44) 0207-241-1991
Web site: www.textilesfromnature.com
Cushions and curtains from organic and eco-friendly fabrics

Zimmer + Rohde

Zimmersmühlenweg 14-16
61440 Oberursel/Frankfurt, Germany
Tel: (49) 6171-632-02
Web site: www.zimmer-rohde.com
To the trade only; silks, transparent fabrics, and pile weaves

---

WINDOWS AND TREATMENTS

Ado International

PO Box 3447
851 Simuel Road
Spartanburg, SC 29304, USA
Tel: (800) 845-0918 (USA);
  (800) 361-5920 (Canada)
Fax: (888) 766-5895 (USA);
  (800) 561-6839 (Canada)
Web site: www.ado-usa.com
Curtains and shades

Pella Corporation

102 Main Street
Pella, IA 50219, USA
Tel: (800) 547-3552
Fax: (515) 628-6457
Web site: www.pella.com
Retractable shades sandwiched between double window panes never need cleaning

Research Frontiers

240 Crossways Park Drive
Woodbury, NY 11797, USA
Tel: (516) 364-1902; (888) SPD-REFR
Fax: (516) 364-3798
Web site: www.refr-spd.com
Developers of suspended particle device (SPD) "smart window" technology that allows users to regulate the amount of light passing through normally clear glass or plastic

Seattle Glass Block

6029 238th Street SE
Woodinville, WA 98072, USA
Tel: (425) 483-9977; (800) 829-9419
Fax: (425) 483-9987

Smith + Noble

Tel: (800) 560-0027
Web site: www.smithandnoble.com
Window blinds in wood, bamboo, and other natural products

PHOTOGRAPHERS

Courtesy of Ado International, 101

Sandy Agrafiotis, 29; 56

Courtesy of Asko, 52

Antoine Bootz, 127

Courtesy of California Closets, 108

Courtesy of Classical Flagstones, 9

Guillaume de Laubier, 145

Guillaume de Laubier/F.J. Graff Design, 116

Carlos Domenech, 66

Carlos Domenech/Keller Donovan, 6 (second from right); 73; 147

Carlos Domenech/Larraz Residence, 37; 142

Carlos Domenech/Roberta Marks, 13

Carlos Domenech/Taylor & Taylor, 11

Carlos Domenech/Wallace Tutts, Tutts Company, 23

Courtesy of Equator, 64

Anna French, Ltd., 90

Courtesy of The Glidden Company, 2; 18 30; 41; 42; 45; 82; 86; 118; 133

Courtesy of Hettich, 54

Courtesy of Ikea, 50; 81

Courtesy of The Kohler Company, 6 (left); 59 (bottom); 105; 107; 113

© Living, Etc./IPC Syndication, 15

Courtesy of Maine Cottage Furniture, 22; 71; 85; 89

Courtesy of Marimekko, 55; 119; 137

© Paul Massey/Living, Etc./IPC Syndication, 21

Eric Roth, 32; 47; 61; 76; 92; 94; 138; 146

Eric Roth/ Tom Catalano Architecture, 103

Eric Roth/Cheryl & Jeffrey Katz Design, 122

Eric Roth/Michael Kirtchmeyer Designs, 100

Greg Premru, 63; 151; 152

Courtesy of R.O.O.M., 70; 75; 95; 129

Courtesy of Smith + Noble, 1; 25; 114

Courtesy of Spiegel, 31; 48; 59 (top); 69; 110

Tim Street-Porter/Andrew Batey Designs, 125

Tim Street-Porter/Nancy Goslee Power Design/www.beat-eworks.com, 121

Brian Vanden Brink, 26; 79; 131; 135; 141

Brian Vanden Brink/Roc Caivano, Architect, 38

Brian Vanden Brink/Tony DiGregorio, Architect, 98

Brian Vanden Brink/Jeremiah Eck, Architect, 35

Brian Vanden Brink/Builder, South Mountain Company, 97

© Mark Williams/Living, Etc./IPC Syndication, 17

Courtesy of Zimmer + Rohde, 149

Special Thanks to:
Clodagh Design International
670 Broadway, 4th Floor
New York, NY 10012
Tel: (212) 780-5307
Fax: (212) 780-5755
Web Site: www.clodah.com

ABOUT THE AUTHOR

Jackie Craven writes about architecture, design, and travel for magazines, newspapers, and Internet services. She is a columnist for *House & Garden* magazine, and she writes the architecture pages for the news and entertainment site, About.com. Passionate about historic buildings, she has restored five old houses on her street in upstate New York. Visit her online at www.jackiecraven.com.